Christoph Rauhut & Niels Lehmann

FRAGMENTS OF METROPOLIS RHEIN & RUHR

Das expressionistische Erbe an Rhein und Ruhr
The Expressionist Heritage of the Rhine-Ruhr Region

HIRMER

Seit über fünf Jahren widmen wir uns dieser Dokumentation zur Architektur des Expressionismus, jene gebaute Avantgarde der Zwischenkriegsjahre, die noch immer nicht in ihrer Gänze erfasst ist und kaum die ihrer Bedeutung zustehende Würdigung erhält. Umso mehr freut es uns, dass nun nach dem ersten Band zu Berlin und Brandenburg unsere Buchreihe mit den »Fragmenten« der Bewegung an Rhein und Ruhr fortgesetzt werden kann. Denn diese Metropolenregion, deren Identität durch den Strukturwandel einiges erdulden musste, besitzt ein besonders glanzvolles Erbe expressionistischer Architektur, das von Stolz und Hoffnung zeugt. Eindrucksvoll ist die große Bandbreite – auch jenseits der Industrieanlagen – mit beachtlichen Beispielen an Kunst-, Sakral- und Kommerzbauten und Gebäuden für das Gemeinwesen. Wir laden ein, diese Zeugen der expressionistischen Utopie wiederzuentdecken. Auf dass Sie vielleicht sogar die eine oder andere Anregung finden – so wie es Alexander Gutzmer im ›Baumeister‹ zum ersten Band schrieb: »Ein bisschen mehr Expressionismus könnte helfen.«

Christoph Rauhut & Niels Lehmann

For over five years we have devoted our-
selves to documenting the architecture of
Expressionism: that built avant-garde of
the interwar years, which even today has
still not been covered in its entirety nor
has its significance found its due appreciation. Thus, it is our great pleasure to
announce that following the first volume
on Berlin and Brandenburg, our series of
publications can be continued with the
"fragments" of the movement in the Rhine
and Ruhr region. This metropolitan region,
whose identity has had to endure much in
the way of structural change, has a particularly glorious legacy of Expressionist architecture, that is a testament of pride and
hope. It has an impressive range of building types — going far beyond the industrial types — with remarkable examples of
buildings that serve art, religion, commerce
and community. With this book, we invite
you to rediscover these witnesses of the Expressionist utopia, with the hope that you
might even find stimulus from what you find
— as Alexander Gutzmer wrote about the
first volume in the journal 'Baumeister': "a
little more Expressionism could be helpful."

Als ich zum ersten Mal in diesem Buch blätterte, überkam mich der Wunsch, hinauszugehen und neu zu entdecken: expressionistische Architektur, deren Existenz »Fragments of Metropolis – Rhein & Ruhr« wieder in unser Bewusstsein rückt. Längst gehört der Expressionismus in anderen Kunstformen zum Kulturkanon – ausgerechnet dort aber, wo er jedem zugänglich ist, geriet er in Vergessenheit. Als Kanzlei des Ruhrgebiets ist es uns ein Anliegen, diesen Schatz der Region wieder sichtbar zu machen: Zum einen, weil die expressionistische Architektur eng verknüpft ist mit den hiesigen Unternehmen, denen wir in langer Tradition verbunden sind. Zum anderen, weil darin eine große Chance liegt: Nur wenn wir vergangene Epochen verstehen, können wir unsere Zukunft sinnvoll gestalten. In Zeiten großer gesellschaftlicher Spannungen und Umbrüche ist es wichtiger denn je, im Neuen die Herausforderung zu erkennen, anzunehmen und zu bewältigen.

Michael Schacke, Partner

KÜMMERLEIN
RECHTSANWÄLTE & NOTARE

As I browsed through this book for the first time, I found myself inspired to go out and discover Expressionist architecture anew: an architecture whose existence "Fragments of Metropolis – Rhein & Ruhr" brings to our attention once again. In other art forms, Expressionism for many years has been part of the cultural canon — but excluded from this was the art form accessible to all: Expressionist architecture was almost forgotten. For a law firm in the Ruhr Region, it is our intent to make this treasure visible again: first, because Expressionist architecture is closely linked to the region's companies, with whom we share a long-standing tradition. Second, because there is much potential in doing so: only when we understand past epochs, we are able to meaningfully shape our future. In times of great social tensions and fractures, it is more important than ever to recognise the challenge of the new; to take it on and to cope with it.

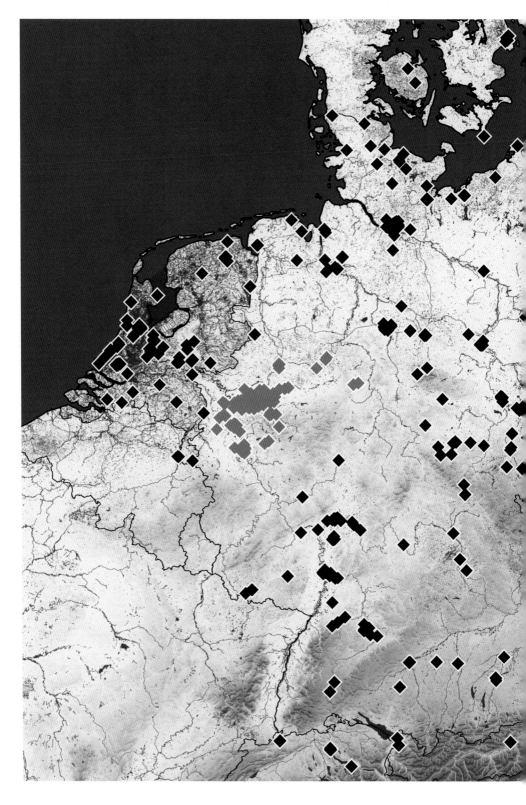

Nord- & Ostsee | North Sea & Baltic, Niederlande | Netherlands,
Berlin (erschienen | published), Rhein & Ruhr, Osteuropa | Eastern
Europe, Mitteldeutschland | Central Germany, Süddeutschland,
Schweiz & Österreich | South Germany, Switzerland & Austria

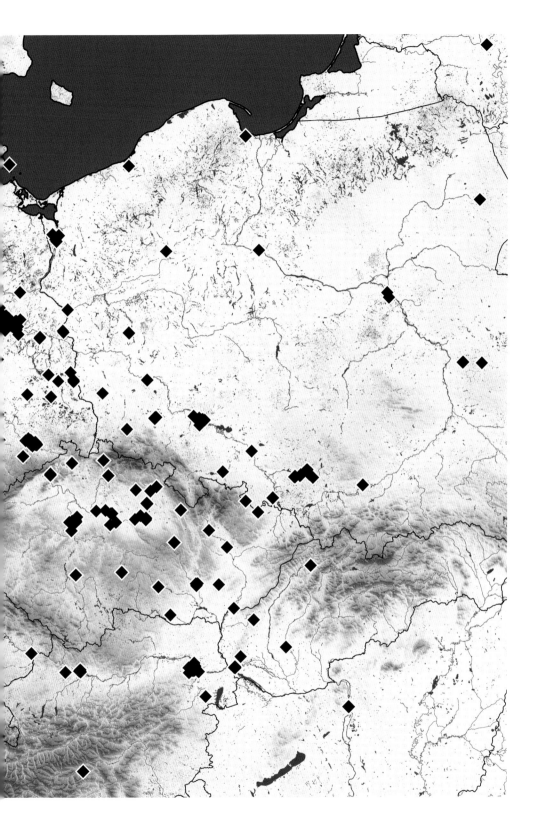

INHALT
CONTENTS

Paul Kahlfeldt

BAUKUNST ALS VORBILD UND ERMAHNUNG

Beim Anblick der hier präsentierten Bauwerke überkommt den Betrachter unwillkürlich eine gewisse Sentimentalität. Durchweg – von den Wohnhäusern über die so bezeichneten Zweckbauten, die Gebäude der Verwaltung bis hin zum Sakralbau – erkennt man einen Willen zur Gestalt, zum Sinn der Form: Die Baumassen sind gegliedert, die Volumen strukturiert und bis in die Feinheiten der Details offenbart sich ein anspruchsvoller architektonischer Ausdruck.

Trotz der Individualität der einzelnen Gebäude bleibt eine gemeinsame Haltung erkennbar und der Zeitraum ihrer Errichtung ist eindeutig. Diesen in einen Begriff zu fassen, liegt nahe und es bietet sich die gewählte Klassifizierung an. »Expressionismus« sollte jedoch nicht als Stilbegriff verstanden werden, denn die Formensprache der Gebäude erinnert vielmehr an eine epochenübergreifende architektonische Gestaltung aus den Gesetzen der Konstruktion, der Materialität und der Gliederung. Es ist dieser spürbare Wille zum baukünstlerischen Ausdruck, der die Verbindung zwischen den Bauten herstellt.

Angesichts des in dieser Zeit am architektonischen Horizont aufsteigenden »Neuen Stils« der abstrahierenden Vereinfachung ist die Besinnung und Konzentration auf handwerkliche und baukünstlerische Regeln nachvollziehbar und dieses bis heute letztmalige gemeinschaftliche Aufbäumen gegen die sich abzeichnende

Banalisierung des Metiers ist bewunderswert
und vorbildlich.

Neben einer autonomen Sprache der Architektur und den für alle Regionen der Welt gel-
tenden Erfordernissen des Bauens zeigen sich in
der Bauweise und Lesbarkeit die regionalen Ein-
flüsse auf die Erscheinung der Bauwerke. Handwerkliche Traditionen und ortstypische Materia-
lien prägen die Form und verantworten das Bild.
Auch wenn die Architekten bereits in dieser Zeit
planerisch nicht mehr an ihren Standort gebun-
den und überregional tätig sind, beeinflussen der
Bauplatz und seine Gebundenheit ihre Entwürfe.
Nicht allein die Verwendung von Backstein gibt
den Bauten ihre Gestalt, sondern Format, Ober-
fläche, Verband und Verfugung bestimmen die
Konstruktion und deren Gestaltung. Aus histori-
scher Kontinuität und in Kenntnis vorbildlicher
Referenzbauten bilden sich Wirkung und Ver-
ständlichkeit der ornamentalen Lösungen. Diese
sind nicht aufgesetzt oder hinzugefügt, sondern
aus den anerkannten Grundsätzen der Baukunst
entwickelt, individuell transformiert und den
neuen Erfordernissen angepasst. Diese Akzeptanz
einer Kontinuität verleiht den Bauwerken eine bis
heute wirksame Anerkennung und Bedeutung.

Sind in Berlin vergleichbare Gebäude oft
auf den umgebenden Stadtraum bezogen und fügen sie sich dort durch die Selbstverständlichkeit
preußischen Backsteinbaus eher harmonisch in
die historisch gewachsene Stadt ein, beeindrucken
im dagegen sich schnell entwickelnden Ruhrgebiet die ökonomische Kraft und ihre daraus
vielfach erwachsende autonome Monumentalität
und Größe der Bauvolumen. In dieser Architektur
manifestierten sich nachvollziehbares Selbstbewusstsein und Stolz. Die Bauten prägen mit ihrer
Erscheinung den Ort und stiften Identität. In
ihrer Individualität bleiben sie dennoch Teil einer
architektonischen Gesellschaft und fügen sich ge-
stalterisch entsprechend ein.

Diese notwendigen Verhaltensregeln
sind aus der Mode gekommen und schlechtes
Benehmen in der Baukunst wird heute besten-
falls nur hingenommen, oftmals sogar befördert
und als zeitgemäß angesehen. Entweder entste-
hen einfachste Kisten mit dünnen Verpackungen
aus Glas, Beton oder Ziegel, deren Auswahl nur
geschmacklichen oder ökonomischen Vorgaben
gelangweilter Entscheider folgt, oder jähzornig

gezackte, eventuell trotzig gekrümmte Basteleien, mit Plastik, Blech und Plexiglas überzogen. Diese architektonische Naivität hat ein weltweit gleichförmiges Mittelmaß zur Folge, dessen erschreckende Ödnis nicht mit immer neuen Ermunterungen zu individueller Selbstdarstellung behoben werden kann.

Die vorgestellten Bauwerke sind somit nicht nur baugeschichtlich wichtige Dokumente für eine vollständige Betrachtung des frühen zwanzigsten Jahrhunderts, sondern sie fügen sich auch ein in die lange Reihe vorbildlicher Leitbauten. Zugleich sind sie eine Ermahnung an die heutigen Architekten, die gestalterischen Erfordernisse an die Baukunst wieder als notwendigen Bestandteil der Arbeit zu erkennen und erneut Bauwerke von bleibender Relevanz zu erschaffen.

Paul Kahlfeldt

ARCHITECTURE AS PARAGON AND ADMONITION

Looking at the buildings presented here, the viewer cannot help being overcome by a certain sentimentality. In all the buildings, whether they are residential, industrial or sacred, we see a consistent desire towards form, towards the meaning of form: The building masses are subdivided; the volumes structured; and a sophisticated architectural expression reveals itself throughout, right down to the intricacies of the details.

Despite the individuality of the buildings, a common approach is still discernible and the era in which they were erected is unmistakeable. So, to classify them all under one term comes naturally. "Expressionism" should not, however, be understood as a style, because the form language of the buildings is rather more reminiscent of an approach to architectural design spanning many epochs, rooted in the principles of construction, materiality and composition. It is this tangible will towards architectural expression that links these buildings with one another.

In light of the "New Style" of abstract simplification that was on the architectural horizon at the time, the consciousness of and focus on the principles of craft and building construction is understandable — even today, this collective rebellion against the looming trivialisation of the metier is admirable and exemplary.

Alongside the autonomous language of architecture and the exigencies of construction that can be found in all regions of the world, one can also read regional influences at work in the appearance and construction techniques used in these structures. Craft traditions and materials typical for the place, including their mode of application, shape the resulting forms, and are responsible for the image. Even though architects of this period were no longer bound to place in their activities, but were rather active across regions, the site itself and everything associated with it still influenced their designs. More than just the fact of using brick, it was the format, the surface qualities, the bond and joints used that gave these structures their particular constructive logic and ultimate form. Out of historical continuity and in acknowledgement of references, ornamental motifs were developed in both their effect and inner logic. These are not mere additions, but rather developed out of the basic principles of construction, uniquely transformed and adapted to new requirements. This acceptance of continuity means that the buildings are unmistakeable and significant even today.

Whilst comparable buildings in Berlin often relate to the urban setting that surrounds them, incorporating themselves almost effortlessly into the historic fabric of the city by virtue of their Prussian brickwork alone, in the Ruhr region, an area that developed rapidly, it is the visible traces of this economic power and the many forms of autonomous monumentality that are most impressive. This architecture manifests an understandable self-confidence and pride.

Through their appearance the buildings largely define the character of the place and strengthen its identity. Despite their individuality they remain part of an architectural society and behave accordingly in their design.

These necessary rules of conduct have largely fallen out of fashion, where today bad behaviour in architecture is at best simply tolerated, but sometimes even promoted and regarded as being contemporary. Either simple boxes are built, thinly packaged in glass, concrete or brick according to the taste or economic considerations of the bored decision-makers; or irascibly jagged, almost defiantly curvaceous assemblages skinned in plastic, sheet metal or Plexiglas. This architectural naivety has resulted in a uniform mediocrity around the world, whose terrifying monotony cannot be fixed by a yet another call for individual self-expression.

The buildings presented here are thus not only an important document for a complete consideration of the architectural history of the early twentieth century, but also join the body of canonical works. At the same time, they are an admonition to architects today to recognise the requirements of the art of building once more as a necessary part of their work, and to begin again to create works of lasting relevance.

Christoph Rauhut

METROPOLIS
AN RHEIN UND RUHR

Vielfalt und Gemeinsames – beides prägt
die Metropolenregion Rhein-Ruhr. Gemeinsam
und prägend ist vor allem die stürmische indust-
rielle Entwicklung, die das urspünglich eher länd-
liche Gebiet im 19. und 20. Jahrhundert zu einer
der städtischsten Regionen Europas transfor-
mierte – Ausgangspunkt war der seit Beginn des
19. Jahrhunderts stark intensivierte Abbau der
Kohle, des schwarzen Goldes der Industriali-
sierung. Gemeinsames und Verbindendes sind
insbesondere auch die Verkehrswege, der Rhein
in Süd-Nord-Richtung und die Handels- und
Güterrouten wie etwa der Hellweg oder seit dem
19. Jahrhundert die diversen Eisenbahnlinien
in Ost-West-Richtung. Gemeinsames und bisweilen Vergessenes ist zudem, dass in der Region in
den 1920er-Jahren ein reiches Erbe expressionistischer Architektur entstand.

Gerade jenes ist aber auch durch die Vielfalt der Region bestimmt, die sich vor allem in den
vielen verschiedenen Akteuren abbildet. Dies sind
die miteinander konkurrierenden Städte – Bochum,
Bottrop, Dortmund, Duisburg, Düsseldorf, Essen,
Gelsenkirchen, Hagen, Köln, Oberhausen und
andere –, aber auch die verschiedenen Regie-
rungsbezirke, die mehreren Bistümer, die diversen
Unternehmen und Verbände oder die unterschied-
lichsten Ausbildungsstätten. Diese Vielfalt zeigt
sich auch in unterschiedlichen lokalen kulturellen
Identitäten – in Orten wie Oberhausen, das im

19. Jahrhundert vom Dorf zur Industriestadt wurde, über wichtige historische Handelsstädte wie etwa Dortmund bis hin zur ehemaligen Residenzstadt Düsseldorf mit ihrem selbstbewussten Bürgertum. Pars pro toto gilt in dieser Region also nur begrenzt, Gemeinsames und auch Eigenes ist als Einstieg in die Beschäftigung mit dieser ereignisreichen Zeit und ihrem Erbe anzusprechen.

In den ersten Jahren nach dem Ersten Weltkrieg glich die Region zunächst vielen anderen Gebieten des ehemaligen deutschen Kaiserreichs: Verschiedene politische Gruppierungen umkämpften die Macht, es gab Separationsbestrebungen wie etwa die Rheinische Republik, Besetzung und Versailler Vertrag waren unliebsame Erinnerungen an den verlorenen Ersten Weltkrieg. Anfang der 1920er-Jahre spitzte sich die politische und wirtschaftliche Lage als Folge des Versailler Vertrags und nicht geleisteter Reparationszahlungen dann in besonderer Weise zu: 1921 besetzten Belgien und Frankreich Duisburg und Düsseldorf, 1923 das ganze Ruhrgebiet. Der durch die preußische Regierung ausgerufene passive Widerstand gegenüber der »Ruhrbesetzung« führte zu einer weiteren Steigerung der Inflationsrate. Aus der bereits seit 1914 herrschenden Inflation wurde die Hyperinflation, die zur Währungsreform von 1924 führte, die dann der verspätete Startschuss in die Goldenen Zwanziger war. Denn paradoxerweise war die (Schwer-)Industrie der Region letztlich gestärkt aus den Folgen des Versailler Vertrags hervorgegangen, weil man tiefgreifende technische Erneuerungen und Rationalisierungen durchgeführt hatte. In dem im Zuge dieser Investitionen in die Region kommenden Kapital lagen die Ursprünge eines Baubooms, der dann in der zweiten Hälfte der Zwanzigerjahre das Bild der Städte an Rhein und Ruhr verändern sollte.

Häufig wird dieses neue Bild mit den großen, heroischen und vielfach auch ästhetisch anspruchsvollen Bauten für die die Region bestimmende Montanindustrie gleichgesetzt. Doch bieten die verschiedenen Städte an Rhein und Ruhr ein weitergehendes, zu entdeckendes architektonisches Erbe der Zwanzigerjahre – mit Bauten für öffentliche Funktionen, für Verwaltung und Administration, für Wohnen, für den Glauben. Die große Klammer dieser Architektur ist der stolze Wunsch eines Fortschritts, der über Kontinuität erreicht werden sollte – eine Haltung, die diese Baukunst bis heute auszeichnet. Spannend ist es, sich die diversen Städte separat anzuschauen, denn überall passierte ganz Eigenes – zumeist getragen von lokalen Protagonisten.

Bochum ist so ein Fall: Hier war es der Architekt Heinrich Schmiedeknecht (1880–1962), der das »expressionistische« Bild der Stadt etwa durch Bauten für den städtischen Nahverkehrsbetrieb (102) oder auch die lokale Industrie (108) besonders prägte. Der gebürtige Bochumer war – für diese Zeit ungewöhnlich – zeitlebens ausschließlich als Privatarchitekt tätig und baute sowohl für institutionelle wie auch private Bauherren. Aufträge erhielt er neben Wettbewerbsteilnahmen vor allem auch direkt von den Bauherren – und bescherte Bochum somit ein äußerst vielseitiges expressionistisches Erbe.

In Oberhausen hingegen lag der Fokus sehr stark auf öffentlichen Bauten beziehungsweise Bauten für die Öffentlichkeit, herausragende Beispiele sind unter anderem das Rathaus (131), zwei Polizeigebäude (106, 145) oder das Kaufhaus Tietz (123). Zentraler Protagonist in Oberhausen war der Stadtbaumeister Ludwig Freitag (1888–1973), der in den Zwanzigerjahren ein Bebauungskonzept für einen neuen Stadtkern entwickelte und teilweise auch selbst umsetzte. Das Rathaus war gewissermaßen der Höhepunkt: Einfache stereometrische Baukörper wurden zu einer Gesamtkomposition gefügt, Muschelkalk nobilitiert horizontal und vertikal gegliederte Fenster, dreiecksförmiges Maßwerk am Dachrand wirkt als Reminiszenz an die Kontinuität handwerklichen Bauens, ein Uhrenturm markiert in gedämpfter Weise die Stadtkrone.

Hagen wiederum ist dadurch gekennzeichnet, dass es eine ganze Reihe von Personen gab, die den Expressionismus der Stadt prägten. So kann die Stadt mit einem äußerst vielseitigen entsprechenden baulichen Erbe aufwarten, das vor allem durch Wohnbauten geprägt ist, aber mit Bauten wie dem Lagerhaus Lehnkering (36) oder der Wagenhalle für die Hagener Straßenbahn AG (78) auch ganz außergewöhne Bauten der Zeit umfasst. Hier wirkte der »Hagener Impuls« nach, der durch den Hagener Kunstmäzen Karl Ernst Osthaus (1874–1921) getragene Versuch, die kleine Industriestadt Anfang des 20. Jahrhunderts zu einem Zentrum des Werkbundes und der Idee eines edlen Zusammenschlusses von Künstlern, (Kunst-)Handwerkern und Industriellen zu machen.

In Düsseldorf und Essen hingen Bauproduktion und vor allem das Architektennetzwerk eng mit den lokalen Ausbildungsstätten zusammen. In beiden Fällen passierten die entscheidenden Weichenstellungen bereits vor dem Ersten Weltkrieg: In Düsseldorf war dies zunächst 1903 die Berufung von Peter Behrens (1868–1940) als Leiter der Kunstgewerbeschule, um, ähnlich wie es in Darmstadt mit Joseph Maria Olbrich (1867–1908) gelungen war, die Stadt an der Spitze der zeitgenössischen Reformbewegung in Kunst und Architektur etablieren zu können, sowie ab 1908 dann die Berufung von Wilhelm Kreis (1873–1955) als dessen Nachfolger. Diese personellen Besetzungen hatten vor allem auch das Ziel, die Architekturabteilung der Gewerbeschule als Gegenpol zur Architektenausbildung an der Kunstakademie zu positionieren. Da der politische Rückhalt aber fehlte, sollte dies nicht gelingen: Behrens verließ Düsseldorf eher enttäuscht, so wie man auch von ihm enttäuscht war, und die Architekturabteilung der Gewerbeschule ging 1919 in der Kunstakademie auf, sodass Kreis dann 1926 nur zu gerne einem Ruf nach Dresden folgte, nachdem auch seine monumentalen, für die Große Ausstellung für Gesundheitspflege, soziale Fürsorge und Leibesübungen, kurz GESOLEI, errichteten Bauten (136, 137, 138, 139) nur wenig Begeisterung auslösten. Doch waren mit Behrens und Kreis Autoritäten nach Düsseldorf gekommen, die als Personen und insbesondere als Lehrer einzelne (lokale) Architekten deutlich beeinflussten. Dies ist insbesondere im Fall von Kreis offensichtlich, der in Düsseldorf lange ein Privatatelier unterhielt. Mitarbeiter waren unter anderem Hans Tietmann (1883–1935) und Karl Haake (1889–1975), die etwa das Düsseldorfer Pressehaus (113) und das Industriehaus am Wehrhahn (117) als Partner bauten.

Ganz anders war die Entwicklung in Essen: Auch Essen wollte als aufstrebende Industrie-, aber auch Wohn- und Verwaltungsstadt zur Jahrhundertwende seine Ausbildungsstätten neu aufstellen. Trotz eines erbitterten Widerstands seitens der Düsseldorfer Bezirksregierung konnte die Stadt die 1901 eröffnete Gewerbeschule immer weiter ausbauen. 1911 gelang ein Doppelschlag: Nicht nur konnte eine staatlich genehmigte Essener Handwerker- und Kunstgewerbeschule gegründet, sondern mit Alfred Fischer (1881–1950) auch einer der führenden Architekten der Zeit als

Leiter gewonnen werden. Zu verdanken war dies
vor allem auch der zeitgenössischen Werkbund-
und Architekten-Instanz Hermann Muthesius
(1861–1927), der in Essen die Chance sah, eine
Musterschule für die Verbindung von preußischen
Bildungsbestrebungen und den Intentionen des
Werkbunds zu gründen. Fischer gelang es, die
Schule vor und nach dem Ersten Weltkrieg zu
einem Zentrum des kulturellen und architektonischen Geschehens der Stadt zu machen, noch
heute steht der 1928 etablierte Name »Folkwang-
Schule« für hohen künstlerischen und gestalterischen Anspruch. Ein zentrales Element war dabei,
dass Fischer auch von Industrie und Handwerk
große Wertschätzung erhielt. Seine Definition des
Gesamtkunstwerks, bei der das Architektonische
im Zentrum des »Organismus« steht, erlaubte
nämlich, dass alle gewerblichen Interessensträger
sich in den Strukturen der Schule wiederfanden.
Über Fischer und die Schule standen die lokalen
Architekturprotagonisten wie der für Essen über-
aus wichtige Architekt Edmund Körner (1874–
1940) oder etwa Georg Metzendorf (1874–1934) in
einem fortwährenden Austausch.

　　　Der Vergleich Düsseldorf–Essen ist auch
insofern interessant, als die Architektur der beiden
zentralen Protagonisten Kreis und Fischer sehr
unterschiedlich zu verorten ist und verschieden
aufgenommen wurde: Mit Kreis versuchte die
Stadt Düsseldorf, ihre Architektur zu aktuali-
sieren. Seine Bauten waren die ersten lokalen
Bauten der Moderne, hatten Reformbewegung
und Jugendstil doch vor dem Ersten Weltkrieg
keinen Erfolg gehabt, zu sehr war man bis auf
einzelne Ausnahmebauten noch dem Duktus
preußisch-monarchischer Prachtentfaltung verhaf-
tet gewesen. Dass Kreis trotzdem beziehungsweise
gerade deshalb mit aristokratischen Motiven wie
einem Ehrenhof arbeitete, brachte ihm vor allem
bei den GESOLEI-Bauten eine erhebliche Kritik
ein. Man empfand seine Architektur nicht als
modern, sondern als restaurativ – sie erinnere
an »ehemalige Festungswerke, [...] nilstromum-
flutete Grabhügelbauten, [...] unfertig gebliebene
italienische Kirchenwände« (Werner Hegemann,
1926). Zudem bemängelte man den hohen Mate-
rialeinsatz bei den zunächst temporär geplanten
Bauten; die monumentale Gestaltung bedinge eine
aufwendige Verblendung eigentlich aufgelöster
Baukonstruktionen. Eine ähnliche Kritik wurde

auch gegenüber den kurz später errichteten Bauten zur »Pressa« (127) in Köln geäußert – die Debatte wurde in der Zeit mehr oder weniger polemisch geführt.

Fischer hatte es hingegen in Essen in zweifacher Hinsicht besser: Zum einen war die Stadt in ihrem Selbstverständnis weit mehr von Zukunftshoffnung als von Traditionspflege bestimmt, zum anderem war Fischers Architektursprache mehrheitsfähiger. Seine gedämpfte, gleichwohl eigenständige Monumentalität als Ausdrucksmittel verkörperte das neue Selbstbewusstsein der aufstrebenden Region. Nicht die rückgreifenden Motive standen im Vordergrund, sondern das moderne Bauen. Zugleich spiegelte sich in den Bauten ein ungeheurer Reichtum architektonischer Gestaltungsansätze und -lösungen wider. Fischer entfaltete deshalb auch eine Vorbildwirkung über die Stadt hinaus in die ganze Metropolenregion.

Ein breiter Überblick über die verschiedenen expressionistischen Bauten an Rhein und Ruhr besticht durch die Unterschiedlichkeit der verwirklichten Gebäude. Zu finden sind private Villen und große öffentliche Verwaltungsbauten, städtebaulich markante Sakralbauten und Relikte ganzer Industrieanlagen. Dies offenbart den architektonischen Expressionismus als ein Breitenphänomen – der aber durchaus mit unterschiedlichen Mitteln aufgegriffen und angewendet wurde und auch Schwerpunkte setzte: So ist ein an Rhein und Ruhr häufig auftretender Gebäudetypus das Wohnhochhaus – wie etwa jenes in Düsseldorf (100) oder die Kopfbauten der dortigen Siedlung Rheinpark (112) – beziehungsweise Wohngebäude, die durch eine besondere Höhenentwicklung städtebaulich markante Situationen schaffen – Beispiele sind das Geschäftshaus Lommel (93) in Hamm oder das Ring-Eck (88) und Sternhaus (89) in Gelsenkirchen. Hier wird das Motiv des Vertikalen, des Aufstrebenden und sich Auflösenden besonders betont. Gewissermaßen auf die Spitze getrieben wurde diese Idee durch den Hochhauswettbewerb, den sich Düsseldorf und Köln in der Zeit lieferten. So war zunächst das als Eisenbetonkonstruktion errichtete Düsseldorfer Wilhelm-Marx-Haus (135) das höchste Bürogebäude Europas, bevor es darin 1925 von dem Kölner Hansaring-Hochhaus (133), ebenfalls einer Eisenbetonkonstruktion, abgelöst wurde. In Konkurrenz stand man zu Städten wie Breslau oder Berlin.

Alle diese »vertikalen« Gebäude sind an wichtigen Kreuzungen, Plätzen oder Fluchten als auffällige Weg- und Identifikationspunkte platziert, sie wurden äußerst planvoll in den Stadtraum gesetzt. Dies aber nicht mit repräsentativem Gestus, sondern vielmehr in der Tradition Camillo Sittes in künstlerisch gestalteter, bisweilen malerischer Manier. In den vielfach in die Fläche wachsenden Städten wollte man mit den Hochhäusern und hohen Häusern auch das Raumbild der dichten Stadt konservieren beziehungsweise wiedergewinnen.

Eine weitere besondere Gruppe sind die Sakralbauten. Beinahe in jeder Stadt sind mehrere expressionistische Beispiele zu finden, die nicht nur vom Bevölkerungswachstum der Zeit zeugen, sondern auch die herausragende Rolle der Kirche, die eine wesentliche kulturpolitische Macht der Region war, als Bauherr dokumentieren. War der Umgang mit der expressionistischen Klaviatur zwar höchst unterschiedlich – so gibt es gotische oder auch romanische Anlehnungen genauso wie formal höchst eigenständige Beispiele, allen voran die Kölner St.-Engelbert-Kirche (92) von Dominikus Böhm (1880–1955) – so eint viele Sakralbauten doch, dass deren expressionistische Architektur auch als ein liturgischer Aufbruch gedeutet werden kann. Das Rheinland war damals ein Zentrum von Reformbewegungen, deren Anliegen vor allem auch die Veranschaulichung und Verlebendigung des liturgischen Handelns waren. Architekten wie Böhm und Rudolf Schwarz (1897–1961), die in engem Austausch mit Protagonisten der Reformbewegungen standen, wirkten als Vermittler in die Architektur. Hier paarten sich dann expressionistische Utopie und christlicher Aufbruch.

Die Fragmente der expressionistischen Begeisterung an Rhein und Ruhr haben eine sehr bewegte Geschichte hinter sich: Manche sind schon als veränderte Wiederaufbauten nach Zerstörungen des Ersten Weltkriegs entstanden, so zum Beispiel das Essener Ruhrhaus (103); viele sind dann durch den Zweiten Weltkrieg zerstört beziehungsweise im Wiederaufbau abgetragen worden, so etwa eine 1927 von Josef Rings (1878–1957) erbaute Festhalle ebenfalls in Essen; einige sind aber auch wiederaufgebaut worden, wie – mit allerdings großen Veränderungen – die Börse in Essen (122). Viele Fragmente wiederum sind uns heute durch Umbauten und Erneuerungen im

Wesentlichen nur noch als Fassaden und Kubatur
erhalten, Beispiele sind etwa die »Pressa«-Ausstel-
lungshalle in Köln (127) oder das Hans-Sachs-Haus
in Gelsenkirchen (134). Fast zu jedem Fragment
gibt es eine Geschichte von Wertschätzung und
Ernüchterung zu erzählen – die Dynamik des
Bestands ist vielfältig und zugleich erschreckend.
Es ist zu hoffen (aber keinesfalls gewiss), dass den
noch existierenden Gebäuden in Zukunft eine
ihnen gebührende Anerkennung zuteil werden
wird. Denn diese Fragmente erzählen von Stolz,
Verantwortungsbewusstsein und Hoffnung – und
bleiben somit aktuell.

Christoph Rauhut

METROPOLIS ON THE RHINE AND RUHR

Diversity and commonality — both shape the Rhine-Ruhr metropolitan region. What they have in common is, above all, the turbulent industrial development that transformed the predominantly rural region over the course of the 19th and 20th centuries into one of the most urbanised regions in Europe. It all began with the great intensification of coal extraction, the black gold of industrialisation. What they also have in common and what connects them is the transport routes: the River Rhine that runs from south to north, and the trade routes such as the mediaeval Hellweg, or, from the 19th century onwards, the many railway lines running East-West. Another thing they share, often forgotten, is the fact that a rich legacy of Expressionist architecture was built in the region during the 1920s.

This legacy is also influenced by the diversity of the region, mainly reflected in the many different actors involved. These include the cities that sought to compete with one another — the likes of Cologne, Bochum, Bottrop, Dortmund, Duisburg, Düsseldorf, through to Essen, Gelsenkirchen, Hagen and Oberhausen, amongst others — but also the various administrative districts, several dioceses, various companies and associations and the most diverse kinds of educational institutions. The diversity is also reflected in different local cultural identities — in places like Oberhausen, which developed from being a village into an industrial city over the course of the 19th century, through to important historical merchant cities such as Dortmund, and to the former royal seat of Düsseldorf with its self-confident middle class. *Pars pro toto* does not hold true for this region; speaking about an eventful period for this region involves commonalities and particularities.

In the years following the First World War, the region initially resembled many other regions of the former German Empire: various political groupings competed for power; there were separatist movements such as the Rhenish Republic; occupation and the Treaty of Versailles were unpleasant memories of defeat in the war. In the early 1920s the political and economic situation that resulted from the Treaty and an unpaid balance of reparations came to a head: in 1921 Belgium and France occupied Duisburg and Düsseldorf, then in 1923 the entire Ruhr region. The passive resistance incited by the Prussian government against the occupation of the Ruhr led to a further increase in the rate of inflation. Out of the inflation that had reigned since 1914 hyper-inflation emerged. This led to the currency reform of 1924, which signalled the delayed start of the Golden Twenties. Paradoxically, the (heavy) industry in the region was ultimately strengthened by the consequences of the Treaty, as far-reaching technical renewal and rationalisation had been carried out as a reaction. In the subsequent movement in capital that came as investment into the region lay the origins of a construction boom, one that was to go on to alter the image of the of the cities on the Rhine and Ruhr in the second half of the 1920s.

Often, this new image is equated with the large, heroic and often carefully composed structures for the coal industry that pervade the region. But the various towns and cities in the Rhine-Ruhr possess a broader architectural legacy from the 1920s – with buildings that served public functions, management and administration and others for housing and for worship. What links all this architecture is the proud desire for progress through continuity, which is also what distinguishes this architecture to this day. It is exciting to look at the various cities separately, as each is quite unlike the other; most of the buildings were built by local protagonists.

Bochum is one such case: it was the architect Heinrich Schmiedeknecht (1880–1962) in particular who formed the 'Expressionist' countenance of the city through buildings such those for the city's local transport network (102) or for local industry (108). It is significant that Schmiedeknecht, who was born in Bochum, worked all his life as a private architect (which was still unusual at that time), yet nevertheless built for both private clients as well as institutional ones. He won work through competitions, but primarily through direct commission. Bochum's expressionistic legacy is extremely versatile as a result.

In Oberhausen on the other hand, the focus is very much on public buildings, more precisely, buildings that serve the public. Outstanding buildings include, amongst others, the Town Hall (131), two Police Stations (106, 145) and the Tietz Department Store (123). The central protagonist in Oberhausen was the city architect Ludwig Freitag (1888–1973), who in the 1920s developed a master plan for a new town centre and realised part by himself. The Town Hall was in a sense the climax: simple masonry volumes are brought together as an overall composition, shell-bearing limestone ennobling horizontally and vertically structured windows, triangular tracery along the eaves acting as a reminder of the continuity of craft building traditions, and a clock tower marking, in subdued fashion, the crown of the city.

In Hagen, we again find a city characterised by a range of people who shaped its Expressionism. Thus the city possesses an extremely diverse Expressionist heritage, mostly characterised by housing, as well as extraordinary buildings of the era such as the Lehnkering Storehouse (36) and the Depot for the Hagener Straßenbahn AG (76). Here we see the effect of the 'Hagener Impulse', the attempt at the beginning of the 20th century by the Hagener art patron Karl Ernst Osthaus (1874–1921) to turn the city into a centre of the German Werkbund, inspired by the idea of a noble association of artists, artisans and industrialists.

In Düsseldorf and Essen, those involved in construction and in particular the network of architects were closely tied to local centres of education. In both cases, the decisive constellation of factors was established before the First World War. In Düsseldorf, these factors included firstly the appointment of Peter Behrens (1868–1940) as director of the Kunstgewerbeschule (School of Arts and Crafts) with the aim of establishing the city at the top of the contemporary reform movement in art and architecture, much as Darmstadt had done through the appointment of Joseph Maria Olbrich (1867–1908); and secondly, the appointment of Wilhelm Kreis (1873–1955) as Behrens' successor in 1908. Above all, this choice was aimed at positioning the architecture department of the School of Arts and Crafts as the counterpoint to the architectural education of the Art Academy. As the political backing was lacking, this aim was not realised: Behrens left Düsseldorf disappointed, with Düsseldorf disappointed with him, and in 1919 the architecture department at the School merged with that of the Art Academy. Kreis, his successor, thus all too happily followed a call to Dresden in 1926, after his monumental buildings for the great exhibition for health care, social care and physical education (in short: GESOLEI) (136, 137, 138, 139) garnered only scant enthusiasm. However, Behrens and Kreis were protagonists, who as employers and especially as teachers significantly influenced individual (local) architects. This is evident especially in the case of Kreis, who long maintained a private studio in Düsseldorf. Amongst others, his employees included Hans Tietmann (1883–1935) and Karl Haake (1889–1975), who later as partners built the Düsseldorf 'Pressehaus' (113) and the Wehrhahn Commercial Building (117).

The development in Essen was quite different: at the turn of the century, as an emerging industrial and administrative centre with a significant population, it also wanted to establish anew its educational institutions. Despite fierce resistance on the part of the Düsseldorf District Government, the city was able to expand continually the School of Trades that had opened in 1901. 1911 saw a twofold success for the city: a state-sanctioned School of Arts and Crafts was founded in Essen, and was fortunate enough to attract Alfred Fischer (1881–1950), one of the leading architects of the period, to become its director. This was especially thanks to the authority of the Werkbund architect Hermann Muthesius (1861–1927), who saw in Essen saw the chance to establish a model school in which Prussian educational efforts and the intentions of the Werkbund could be combined. In the period before and after the First World War Fischer managed to turn the school into a centre of cultural (architectural) events in the city; even today the name of the 'Folkwang School', first coined in 1928, represents high standards of artistic and design achievement. Central to this was that Fischer's efforts were highly valued by both industry and the crafts. His definition of the *Gesamtkunstwerk*, in whose 'organism' architecture was central, allowed each of the trades that had a stake in the school to find their place within its structure. Beyond Fischer and the school were the local architectural protagonists who participated in an on-going exchange, such as Edmund Körner (1874–1940), who was particularly significant for Essen, and Georg Metzendorf (1874–1934).

The comparison between Düsseldorf and Essen is interesting inasmuch as the works of the two central protagonists, Kreis and Fischer, were received in very different ways, and are to be understood differently: In Kreis, the city of Düsseldorf attempted to bring their architecture up to date. His buildings were the first local buildings of modernity, as the reform movement and Art Nouveau had had no successes in the city: it had for too long been held captive by Prussian monarchical splendour (apart from a few individual exceptions). Despite this — or was it for this very reason? — he worked with aristocratic motifs such as the Cour d'honneur, which, especially in the GESOLEI buildings, brought him significant criticism. His architecture was seen not as being modern, but rather as a form of restoration: it was reminiscent of "former fortifications, [...] burial mound structures of the Nile Valley, [...] walls left unfinished in an Italian church" (Werner Hegemann, 1926). Some also criticised the amount of material employed for buildings that were initially intended as temporary; the monumental form necessitated an elaborate cladding that unified its separate structures. Similar criticism was directed at the structures built later for 'Pressa' in Cologne (**127**) — a criticism that was part of a polemic debate being held at that time.

In Essen, Fischer enjoyed a better situation in two respects: firstly, the city's self-understanding was shaped far more by a hope for the future than by obligation to tradition; secondly, Fischer's architectural language was more capable of being popularly accepted. His muted, original monumental means of expression embodied the new self-confidence of the emerging region. Rather than motives harking back to the past, it was modern construction that was the main focus. At the same time, a tremendous wealth of architectural design approaches and solutions is reflected in the buildings. Thus, Fischer had the effect of being a role model for the city and for the whole metropolitan region.

In making a survey of the many Expressionist buildings in the Rhine–Ruhr region, it is impressing to note the diversity of the buildings actually realised. There are private villas and large public administration buildings, religious buildings located within the cities and relics of entire industrial plants. This reveals Expressionism in architecture as a wide-ranging phenomenon — one that was, however, taken up with different means, applied in different ways and with different emphases.

Typical building types in the region include that of the residential tower — such as the one in Düsseldorf (100) or the end-of-row building at the Rheinpark development (112) — as well as buildings that create striking urban situations through arrangements of heights — such as the Lommel House (93) in Hamm, the 'Ring-Eck' (88) and the Star House (89) in Gelsenkirchen. In these works, the motives of the vertical, the aspiring, and the disruptive are particularly emphasised. This idea was taken to the extreme through an ongoing tower-building competition between Düsseldorf and Cologne at the time. Thus, Düsseldorf's Wilhelm Marx Building (135) was Europe's tallest building before Cologne's Hansaring Highrise (133) took its place in 1925 (both were iron-reinforced concrete structures), and both competed with cities such as Breslau (now Wroclaw) and Berlin.

All these 'vertical' buildings are located at important junctions, squares or axes, as noticeable points of orientation or identification, placed very deliberately within the cities. This is done not as a desire for prominence, but rather in the tradition of Camillo Sitte, in forms that involve an artistic, almost painterly manner. In cities that were expanding outwards, the purpose of the tall buildings was also to conserve, or regain, the image of the dense urban centres.

Another particular group is that of the religious buildings. In almost every city we can find several examples of Expressionist architecture that not only bear witness to the growing population of the period, but also document the outstanding role of the church as a client that was still the main cultural power in the region. Whilst the Expressionist repertoire was employed in the most diverse ways – we find Gothic or Romanesque references as often as formally original examples (most spectacularly in the case of St Engelbert Church in Cologne (92) by Dominikus Böhm (1880–1955) – nonetheless, what many religious buildings have in common is that their Expressionist architecture can be interpreted as a liturgical upheaval. At that time the Rhineland was a centre of the reform movement, whose concerns were primarily the exemplification and reanimation of liturgical action. Architects such as Böhm and Rudolf Schwarz (1897–1961), who were in close exchange with protagonists of reform movements, acted as translators of the movement's ideas into architecture. These buildings coupled Expressionist utopia and Christian departure.

The fragments of the Expressionist enthusiasm on the Rhine and Ruhr have a very dynamic history behind them: Some exist today having already been rebuilt after destruction in the First World War, such as the Ruhrhaus (103) in Essen; many were destroyed in the Second World War, or demolished in the reconstruction, such as the Festival Hall, also in Essen, built by Josef Ring (1878–1957); a few were also rebuilt, including (but with significant alterations) the Stock Exchange (122), yet again in Essen. Many fragments remain with us today in the form of conversions and renovations, only as façades and outer surfaces, for example, the 'Pressa' exhibition hall in Cologne (127) and the Hans Sachs Building in Gelsenkirchen (134). Almost every fragment tells a story of appreciation and disenchantment; the vitality of the building stock is varied and at the same time terrifying. We can only hope (without certainty) that the surviving buildings will one day be given the recognition that they are due. For these fragments speak of pride, a sense of responsibility and hope – and so remain relevant.

DIE FRAGMENTE
THE FRAGMENTS

Das Ruhrgebiet war bis zum Kriege das Stiefkind unter den deutschen Bezirken. [...] Aber seit dem Kriege beginnt allmählich und immer stärker sich durchsetzend ein neues Geschlecht, seine breiten und wuchtigen Bauten mitten in diese Trostlosigkeit hineinzusetzen und damit werden nun Kristallationspunkte geschaffen, die einer neuen Kultur dienen werden.

Agnes Waldstein (Kuratorin Museum Folkwang, Essen), 1929

Before the Ruhr was the poor relation amongst the German regions. [...] But since the war a new creed has begun to assert itself, incrementally and with ever greater strength, setting down its broad and powerful buildings in the middle of this desolation, which will serve as focal points for a new culture.

Agnes Waldstein (Curator, Museum Folkwang, Essen), 1929

1
Denkmal Carl Gustav Rommenhöller | Carl Gustav Rommenhöller
Memorial, Schmechtener Straße, Bad Driburg (A), 1932

2
Wasserturm Frillendorf | Frillendorf Water Tower, Ernestinenstraße,
Essen (E), Edmund Körner, 1925–26

3
Umspannwerk Niehl | Niehl Transformer Station, Geestemünder Straße,
Sankt-Leonardus-Straße, Köln | Cologne (A), Adolf Abel?, 1928

4
Villa Andreas Ballin | Villa Andreas Ballin, Elisenstraße 19, Gelsen-
kirchen (F), Josef Franke, 1924–25

0   20

5
Villa Fritz Steinert | Villa Fritz Steinert, Kliedbruchstraße 67, Krefeld (A),
Hans Poelzig, Marlene Poelzig geb.|née Moeschke, 1929?–31?

0 ⸻ 20

6
Schwanentorbrücke | Schwanentor Bridge, Schwanentor, Duisburg (A),
Hans-Siegfried Persch, 1950

7
Portalanlage Hauptfriedhof | Gates, Central Cemetery, Zeppelin-
straße 130–136, Mülheim (A), Theodor Suhnel, 1924

8
Hauptfriedhof | Central Cemetery, Am Gottesacker, Dortmund (A),
Heinrich Strunck, Josef Wentzler, 1920–24

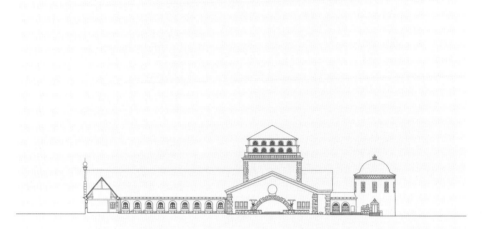

0   20

8
Hauptfriedhof | Central Cemetery, Am Gottesacker, Dortmund (A),
Heinrich Strunck, Josef Wentzler, 1920–24

9
Villa Albert Schwarz, Marienburger Straße 53, Köln | Cologne (A),
Fritz Fuß, 1924–25

10
Villa, Kamener Straße 44, Werne (A)

11
Villa, Schlossparkstraße 14, Düsseldorf (A), Hubert Stupp, 1925

12
Villa Jovy (Volkshochschule | Adult Education Centre), Friedrich-
straße 55, Gladbeck (A), 1927–28

13
Volkshaus Rotthausen | Rotthausen People's House, Grüner Weg 3,
Gelsenkirchen (F), Alfred Fischer, 1920

Villa, Erlestraße 72, Gelsenkirchen (A), Carl Dellweg, 1927

15

Eckhäuser Siedlung Repelen | Corner Houses, Repelen Housing
Estate, Freiligrathstraße, Kamper Straße, Moers (A), 1930–36

16

Gemeindehaus Wanne-Eickel (St. Petrus und Paulus Syrisch-Ortho-
doxe Kirche) | Wanne-Eickel Parish House (Ss Peter and Paul Syriac
Orthodox Church), Deutsche Straße 1, Herne (F), Carl Breuer,
1927–28

17

Die Bastei | Bastei Restaurant, Konrad-Adenauer-Ufer 80, Köln |
Cologne (H), Wilhelm Riphahn, 1924

Villa, Haydnstraße 36, Düsseldorf (A), Hubert Stupp, 1927–28

19
Villa, Haydnstraße 26, Düsseldorf (A), Hubert Stupp, 1928–30

St. Apollinaris | St Apollinaris, St.-Apollinaris-Weg, Lindlar (A),
Dominikus Böhm, 1926–28

St. Apollinaris | St Apollinaris, St.-Apollinaris-Weg, Lindlar (A),
Dominikus Böhm, 1926–28

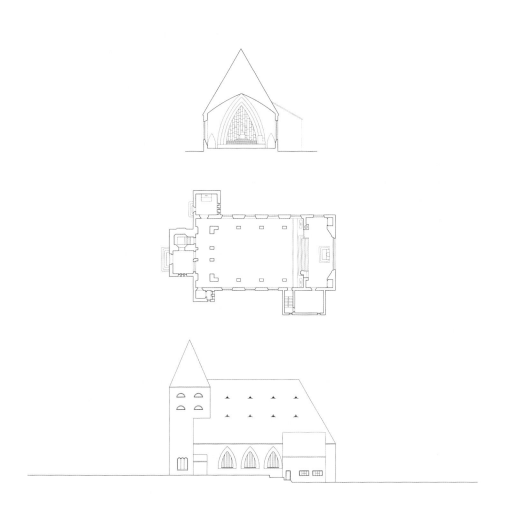

0   20

Bolder Haus | Bolder Building, Koblenzer Straße 65, Köln |
Cologne (A), 1920er? | 1920s?

22
Restaurant Ruhrmann (Wohnhaus) | Ruhrmann Restaurant (House),
Am Stadtgarten 18, Laurentiusweg 75, Essen (A), ca. 1925

23
Siedlung Cunohof | Cunohof Housing Estate, Cunosiedlung, Hagen (G),
Heinrich Balser, Walter Büchsenschütz, Ewald Wachenfeld, Peter
Wiehl, Hans Woltmann, 1926–28

24

Siedlung Auf dem Krahenbrink | Auf dem Krahenbrink Housing
Estate, Georg-Scheer-Straße, Heidestraße, Hagen (A), Otto de Berger,
Eugen Friedrich, 1927–29

25
Wohnhäuser | Flats, Königstraße 28–36, Hagen (G), Josef Demuth,
Hans Köhler, 1928

26
Amtsgericht | District Court, Alter Postweg 36, Dorsten (A),
Hugo Wittneben, 1927–29

27
Jahnschule | Jahn School, Dortmunder Straße 170, Hamm (A),
Wilhelm Eckenrath, 1927–28

28
Wohnhaus | Flats, Stöckstraße 106, Herne (F)

Christuskirche | Church of Christ, Bahnhofstraße 156, Herten (A),
Willy Wolschina, 1933–34

30
Luftschacht Zeche Preußen II (Luftschacht Rote Fuhr) | Ventilation
Tower, Preußen II Mine (Rote Fuhr Ventilation Tower), Rote Fuhr 70,
Dortmund (A), 1925–27

31
Wasserturm | Water Tower, Am Wasserturm 54, Tönisvorst (A), 1920

32

St. Michael | St Michael, Am Trappen 1a, Bochum (A), Anton
Meister, 1925–26

33
Lager- und Bürogebäude Stinnes-Eisenlager GmbH | Stinnes GmbH
Storehouse and Offices, Graf-Beust-Allee 37, Essen (E), Emil Fahren-
kamp, 1922

34
Kokerei Alma | Alma Coking Plant, Almastraße 81/87, Gelsen-
kirchen (F), Fritz Schupp, Martin Kremmer, 1927–28

35
Umspannwerk | Transformer Station, Uferstraße 2–4, Reckling-
hausen (A), Carl Lill, 1927–28

Lagerhaus Lehnkering | Lehnkering Storehouse, Berliner Straße 14,
Hagen (G), Heinrich & Leopold Ludwigs, 1911

37
Lutherkirche | Luther Church, Martin-Luther-Straße 12, Datteln (A),
Hugo Pfarre, Heinrich Strunck, Josef Wentzler, 1927–28

38

Bürohaus »Bochumer Verein« | 'Bochumer Verein' Offices, Essener
Straße 197, Bochum (A), Wilhelm Kreis, 1923

39
St. Michael | St Michael, Falkensteinstraße 234, Oberhausen (J), Fritz
Sonnen, 1928–29

40

Christus-König-Kirche | Church of Christ the King, Klein-Erken-
schwicker-Straße 122, Oer-Erkenschwick (A), Josef Franke, 1928–29

Feuerwache | Fire Station, Bernhard-Ernst-Straße 12, Münster (I),
Felix Sittel, 1928–29

Schulen der Brede | Brede Schools, Bredenweg 7, Brakel (A)

43
Rheinbahnhaus (Betriebshof Heerdt) | Rheinbahn Building (Heerdt
Depot), Kevelaerer Straße 1–5, Düsseldorf (A), Eduard Lyonel
Wehner, 1928–29

44
Geistschule | Geist School, Grevingstraße 24, Münster (I), Karl
Schirmeyer, Felix Sittel, 1929

45
Umbau Dinnendahlsche Fabrik | Conversion, Dinnendahl Factory,
Westfalenstraße 3, Kunstwerkerstraße 179–183, Essen (A), Bernhard
Wielers?, ca. 1925

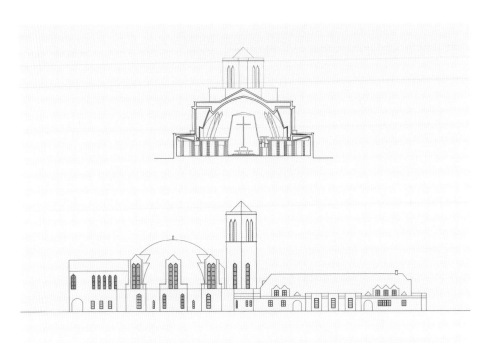

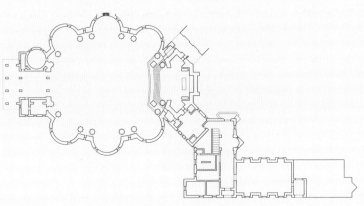

46
Heilige Schutzengel | Church of the Holy Guardian Angels, Auf der
Litten 71, Essen (E), Edmund Körner, 1923–28

47
St. Bonifatius | St Boniface, Max-Brandts-Straße 1, Düsseldorf (D),
Franz Schneider, 1927–28

48

Postamt Buer | Buer Post Office, Königswiese 1, Gelsenkirchen (A),
1927–28

49

Rathaus Brauweiler | Brauweiler Town Hall, Konrad-Adenauer-Platz,
Pulheim (A), Steinberger?, 1926–27

50
Kohlenhandelsgesellschaft Mark (Stadtverwaltung) | Mark Coal
Trading Company (City Administration), Gerichtsstraße 25,
Hagen (G), Ernst Kohlhage, 1925–26

51

August-Thyssen-Realschule | August Thyssen Secondary School,
August-Thyssen-Straße 43, Duisburg (A), 1928–34

52
Wohn- und Geschäftshaus | Flats and Shops, Benrodestraße 90,
Düsseldorf (A)

53
Wohnhaus Nerche | Nerche Flats, Cimbernstraße 3–5, Düsseldorf (D),
Wilhelm Hoppe, 1927–28

54

Paketpost- und Telegrafenamt Wanne-Eickel (Postamt Wanne) |
Wanne-Eickel Parcel Post and Telegraph Office (Wanne Post Office),
Wanner Straße 25, Herne (F), Karl Lachmann, 1932

55
Wohnhaus | Flats, Markgrafenstraße 66, Düsseldorf (D), Wilhelm
Hoppe, 1928

56
Siedlung Lenteninsel | Lenteninsel Housing Estate, Günther-
straße 116–128, Klönnestraße 51–79, Lenteninsel 1–20, Lüne-
burgerstraße 4–24, Dortmund (C), Dietrich & Karl Schulze, 1928

57
Wohnhäuser | Flats, Blumendelle 26–28, Liebfrauenstraße 43–55,
Gelsenkirchen (F), Josef Franke, 1926?

58

Reichsbank Buer | Buer National Bank, Goldbergstraße 14, Gelsen-
kirchen (A), 1926–27

59
Freiherr-vom-Stein-Gymnasium | Freiherr von Stein Scondary School,
Friedenstraße 12, Lünen (A), Dietrich & Karl Schulze, 1929–31

60

Kapelle St. Elisabeth Krankenhaus | Chapel, St Elizabeth Hospital,
Cranger Straße 226, Gelsenkirchen (A), Hubert Kötting, 1925

Heiligste Dreifaltigkeit | Church of the Most Holy Trinity, Magdale-
nenstraße 47, Gelsenkirchen (F), Josef Franke, 1924–26

61

Heiligste Dreifaltigkeit | Church of the Most Holy Trinity, Magdale-
nenstraße 47, Gelsenkirchen (F), Josef Franke, 1924–26

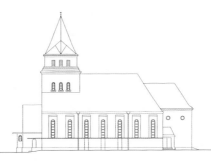

0   20

Evangelisch Stiftisches Gymnasium | Evangelical Monastery Secon-
dary School, Feldstraße 13, Gütersloh (A), Gustav Kassbaum, Paul
Raikowsky, 1926–28

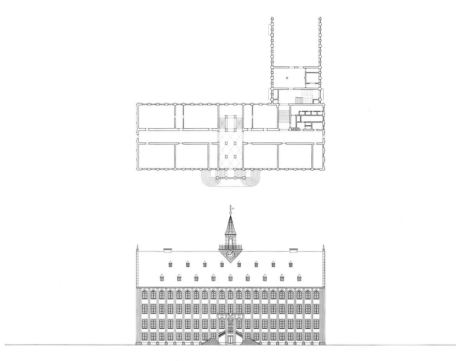

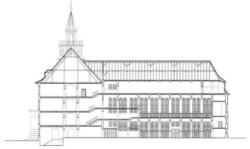

62
Evangelisch Stiftisches Gymnasium | Evangelical Monastery Secon-
dary School, Feldstraße 13, Gütersloh (A), Gustav Kassbaum, Paul
Raikowsky, 1926–28

63
Schule am Tippelsberg | Tippelsberg School, Hiltroper Straße 53,
Bochum (B), Sepp Spannmacher, 1926–28

Christ-König-Kirche | Church of Christ the King, Overbergstraße 67,
Hagen (G), Peter Wiehl, 1928

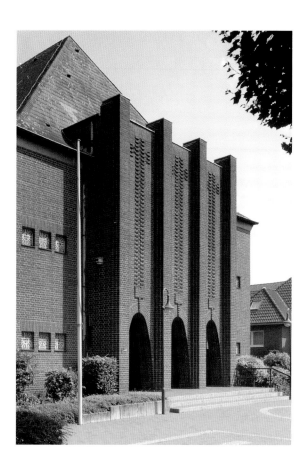

St. Ludgerus | St Ludger, Birkenstraße 75, Bottrop (A), Josef Franke,
1927–29

66

Christuskirche | Church of Christ, Friedrich-Heinrich-Allee 22,
Kamp-Lintfort (A), Arno Eugen? Fritsche, 1928–30

67

Allgemeine Brennstoff-Handelsgesellschaft Camperbruch (ABC-
Gebäude) | Camperbruch Fuel Trading Company (ABC Building),
Ringstraße 130, Kamp-Lintfort (A), 1923?

68

Wohnhäuser | Flats, Esenbeckstraße 1–7, Riehler Gürtel 66–72,
Köln (H), Ernst Wilhelm Scheidt, ca. 1930

69

Wohnhäuser | Flats, Steinmetzstraße 4–12, Goebenstraße 2–14,
Bismarckstraße 1, Bahnhofstraße 141–145, Herne (A), 1922–24

Colonie Werse-Delstrup | Werse-Delstrup Flats, Von-der-Tinnen-
Straße 5–9, Münster (I), 1925–27

71
Wohnhaus | Flats, Mollstraße, Hagen (G), Hans & Max Woltmann,
1922–25

72

Wohnhäuser | Flats, Bülowstraße 16–20, Düsseldorf (D), Joseph
Schönen, 1925–26

73
Wohnhäuser | Flats, Engerstraße 21, Lichtstraße 15, Düsseldorf (A),
Bornheim & Rogge, 1927–28

Wohnhäuser | Flats, Engerstraße 8–10, Düsseldorf (A), Julius Stobbe,
1922–23

75
Berufsschule (Berufskolleg) | Vocational School (Vocational College),
An der Berufsschule 20, Bottrop (A), Albert Lange, 1929

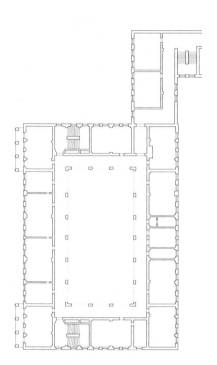

0   20

76
Straßenbahndepot | Tramway Depot, Hauptstraße 55–59, Gelsen-
kirchen (F), Josef Franke, Edmund Körner, 1925

77
Wohnhäuser | Flats, Elbersufer, Hagen (G), Hans & Max Woltmann,
1922–25

78

Wagenhalle Hagener Straßenbahn AG (Lagerhaus Hugo Petri) |
Hagener Straßenbahn AG Depot (Hugo Petri Storehouse), Eckeseyer
Straße 34, Hagen (G), Paul Langensiepen, Hermann Schluckebier,
1927–28

79
Polizeiamt Hamborn | Hamborn Police Station, August-Thyssen-
Straße 39, Duisburg (A), Schultze, 1926–28

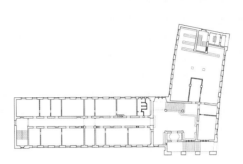

0   20

Volksschule Sülzgürtel (Theodor-Heuss-Realschule) | Sülzgürtel Elementary School (Theodor Heuss Secondary School), Euskirchener Straße 50, Köln (A), Hubert Ritter, ca. 1923

81
Wohn- und Geschäftshaus | Flats and Shops, Bebelstraße 12–14,
Neustraße 19–21, Herne (F), Karl Veuhoff, 1926–28

82

Turm St. Joseph und Medardus | Tower, St Joseph and Medard,
Jockuschstraße 12, Lüdenscheid (A), Joseph Lamm, 1924–28

83

Heilig-Kreuz-Kirche | Holy Cross Church, Liebigstraße 49, Dortmund (C), Hans Homann, 1914–16

84
Polizeipräsidium | Police Headquarters, Uhlandstraße 35, Bochum (B),
Ludwig Scheibner, 1927–29

Wohnhäuser | Flats, Uerdinger Straße 318–322, Krefeld (A)

86

Marktschule Ickern | Ickern School, Kirchstraße 56, Castrop-
Rauxel (A), Alfred Fischer, 1922–26

87
St. Dreikönigen | Church of the Three Kings, Weißdornweg 91,
Köln | Cologne (A), Hans Peter Fischer, Heinrich Forthmann?,
1928–29

Ring-Eck | 'Ring-Eck', Ringstraße 93, Weberstraße 70–72, Gelsen-
kirchen (F), Josef Franke, 1927

0 ━━┕╌┙━━ 20 ◯

89

Sternhaus | Star House, Bismarckstraße 49–51, Hauptstraße 80,
Gelsenkirchen (F), Theodor Waßer, 1926–27

90

Hauptverwaltung Siedlungsverband Ruhrkohlenbezirk (Hauptver-
waltung Regionalverband Ruhr) | Head Offices, Siedlungsverband
Ruhrkohlenbezirk (Head Offices, Regionalverband Ruhr), Kronprinzenstraße 35, Essen (E), Alfred Fischer, 1928–29

91

Stadtsparkasse mit Wohnhäusern (Der Rote Block) | Savings Bank
with Flats (Red Block), Amtmann-Winter-Straße 1–9, Haupstraße 224,
Wibbeltstraße 7–8, Wanner Straße 6–12, Herne (F), Georg Gobrecht,
Ferdinand Revermann, 1926–29

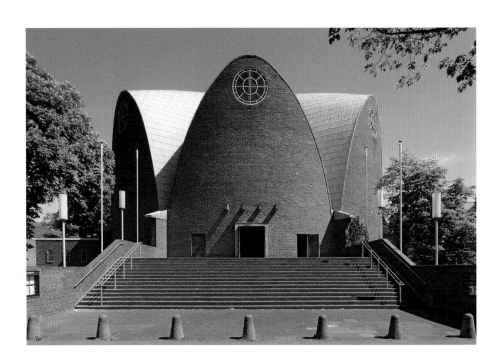

St. Engelbert | St Engelbert, Garthestraße 15, Köln | Cologne (H),
Dominikus Böhm, 1930–32

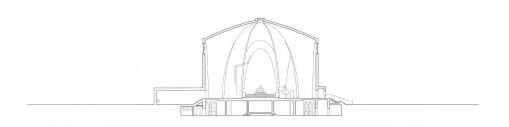

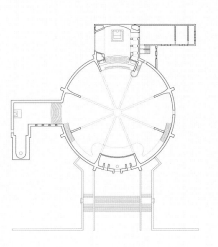

0   20

93
Geschäftshaus Lommel | Lommel House, Weststraße 52, Hamm (A),
Max Krusemark, 1927

94
Wohnhaus | Flats, Emilienplatz, Mollstraße, Hagen (G), August
Keydel

95
Verlagshaus Koethers & Röttsches (Buchhandlung Koethers & Rött-
sches) | Koethers & Röttsches Publishing House (Koethers & Rött-
sches Bookshop), Bebelstraße 18, Herne (A), Josef Kraus, 1926–28

96

Geschäfts- und Bürogebäude | Shops and Offices, Am Markt 26,
Castrop-Rauxel (A)

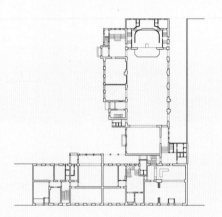

 0   20

97
Kreuzhof | 'Kreuzhof', Essener Straße 8–10, Dortmund (C), Wilhelm
Eckenrath, Wilhelm Schurig, vor | before 1928

98

Wohnhäuser | Flats, Planetenstraße 1–11, 4–10, Suitbertusstraße 38–50,
Düsseldorf (D), Otto Engler, Fritz Hofmeister, Gotthold Nestler, 1927

99

Wohnhäuser [Teil der Siedlung Michaelhof] | Flats [Part of Michael-
hof Housing Estate], Karolingerstraße 28–34, Düsseldorf (D), Otto
Engler, 1927–28

Wohnhochhaus | Residential Tower, Prinz-Georg-Straße 100, Düssel-
dorf (D), Gustav August Munzer, 1927

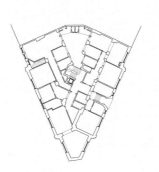

0   20 ⏀

0   20 ⊘

101

Wohnhäuser | Flats, Kaiserswerther Straße 162–166, Golzheimer
Platz 5, 9, Düsseldorf (D), Fritz Becker, Erich Kutzner, 1924–25

BOGESTRA Verwaltungsgebäude | BOGESTRA Offices, Universi-
tätsstraße 54, Bochum (B), Heinrich Schmiedeknecht, 1925–28

103
Ruhrhaus (Verwaltungsgebäude Ruhrverband) | Ruhr Building
(Ruhrverband Offices), Kronprinzenstraße 37, Essen (E), Georg
Metzendorf, Jacob Schneider, 1921?–28?

104

Polizeidirektion | Police Headquarters, Hohe Straße 80, Hamm (A),
Humpert, Oelmann, 1926–28

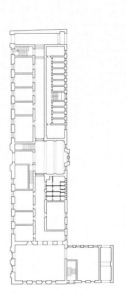

0   20

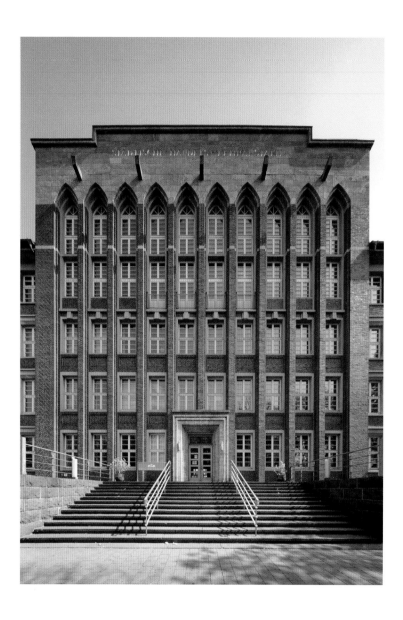

105

Städtische Handelslehranstalten (Hansa-Berufskolleg) | Municipal
Vocational Business School (Hansa Vocational College), Hansaring 80, Münster (I), Felix Sittel, 1928–29

106

Polizeipräsidium | Police Headquarters, Friedensplatz 2–5, Ober-
hausen (J), Ludwig Freitag, 1924–26

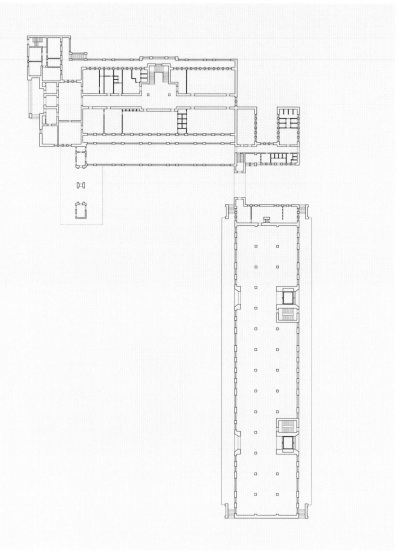

o ⌐_⌐_⌐ 20 ◔

107
Lagerhaus und Verwaltungsgebäude Gutehoffnungshütte | Good Hope
Mine Storehouse and Offices, Essener Straße 80, Oberhausen (J),
Peter Behrens, 1920–25

107
Lagerhaus und Verwaltungsgebäude Gutehoffnungshütte | Good Hope
Mine Storehouse and Offices, Essener Straße 80, Oberhausen (J),
Peter Behrens, 1920–25

108

Siloturm Schlegel-Scharpenssel-Brauerei | Silo Tower, Schlegel
Scharpenssel Brewery, Am Schlegelturm, Bochum (B), Heinrich
Schmiedeknecht, 1927

109

Verwaltungsgebäude Firma Henkel | Henkel Group Offices, Henkel-
straße 67, Düsseldorf (A), Walter Furthmann, 1927–29

110
Herz-Jesu-Kirche | Church of the Sacred Heart, Prosperstraße 32,
Bottrop (A), Josef Franke, 1927–29

St. Kamillus | St Camillus, Kamillianerstraße 40, Mönchenglad-
bach (A), Dominikus Böhm, 1929–31

112
Siedlung Rheinpark | Rheinpark Housing Estate, Kaiserswerther
Straße, Theodor-Heuss-Brücke, Düsseldorf (D), William Dunkel, 1928

113

Pressehaus | 'Pressehaus', Martin-Luther-Platz 26, Düsseldorf (D), Karl
Haake, Hans Tietmann, 1925–26

114
Türme St. Antonius | St Antoninus Towers, Am Schillerplatz 12,
Gelsenkirchen (F), Josef Franke, 1923–28

115
Finanzamt | Tax Office, Schürmannstraße 7, Hagen (G), Alfred
Reischig, 1925–26

Friedrich-Lueg-Haus (Union Kino) | Friedrich Lueg Building (Union
Cinema), Kortumstraße 16, Bochum (B), Emil Pohle, 1924–25

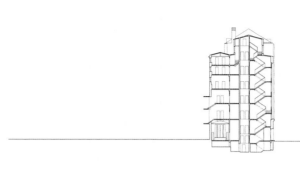

0   20

117
Industriehaus am Wehrhahn | Wehrhahn Commercial Building,
Schirmerstraße 80, Düsseldorf (D), Karl Haake, Hans Tietmann,
1921–23

0   20 ⌐

Danat-Bank | Danat Bank, Königsallee 4, Düsseldorf (D), Albert
Betten, Carl Moritz, 1924

119

Sudhaus Brauerei Müser (Discothek Matrix) | Brewhouse, Müser
Brewery (Matrix Discotheque), Hauptstraße 200, Bochum (A),
Emil Moog, 1927–28

Reichspostdirektion (Hauptpost) | Post Directorate (Main Post Office),
Hachestraße 2–4, Essen (E), Wilhelm Hoeltz, Lindemann, 1924–25,
1933

Reichsbahn-Wasserturm Dortmund-Süd | South Dortmund State
Railway Water Tower, Heiliger Weg 60, Dortmund (C), H. Lehmann,
M. Venner, 1923–27

Börse (Haus der Technik) | Stock Exchange (Technology House),
Hollestraße 1, Essen (E), Edmund Körner, 1922–27 (Wiederaufbau |
Reconstruction, Alfred Pegels 1953)

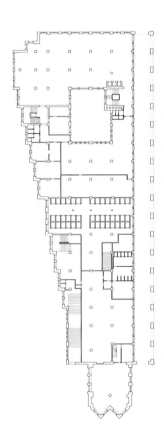

0 ————————— 20

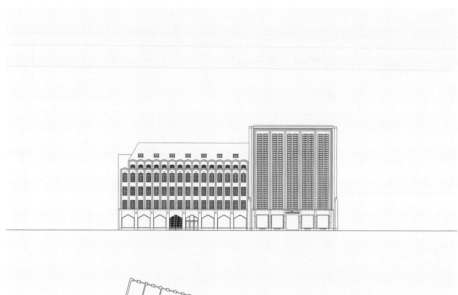

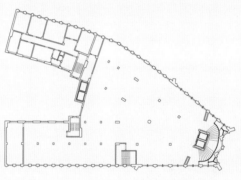

123, 124

Kaufhaus Tietz (Bert-Brecht-Haus), Verlagshaus Ruhrwacht | Tietz
Departement Store (Bert Brecht Building), Ruhrwacht Publishing
House, Langemarkstraße 15–21, Paul-Reusch-Straße, Oberhausen (J),
Otto Scheib, 1925–28, 1925–26

123
Kaufhaus Tietz (Bert-Brecht-Haus) | Tietz Departement Store (Bert
Brecht Building), Langemarkstraße 19–21, Paul-Reusch-Straße,
Oberhausen (J), Otto Scheib, 1925–28

124
Verlagshaus Ruhrwacht | Ruhrwacht Publishing House, Langemark-
straße 15–17, Oberhausen (J), Otto Scheib, 1925–26

125

Erweiterung St. Johannes-Hospital | Extension, St John's Hospital, An
der Abtei 7–9, Duisburg (A), Carl Brocker, 1925–26

126

Verwaltungsgebäude Stumm-Konzern | Stumm Group Offices, Breite
Straße 67–69, Düsseldorf (D), Paul Bonatz, 1922–25

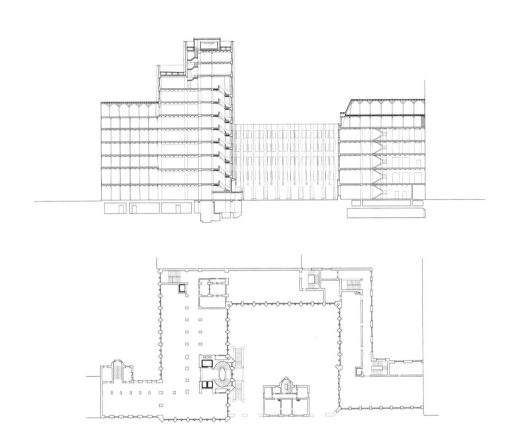

0   20

127
»Pressa«-Ausstellungshalle (Alte Messe) | 'Pressa' Exhibition Hall
(Old Fair), Charles-de-Gaulle-Platz, Köln | Cologne (H), Adolf Abel,
1927–28

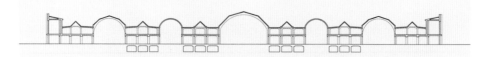

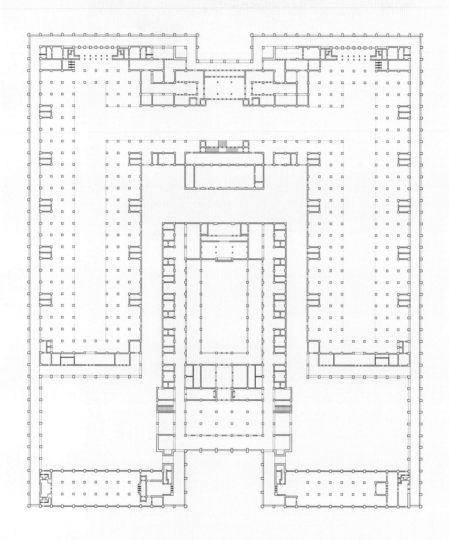

127

»Pressa«-Ausstellungshalle (Alte Messe) | 'Pressa' Exhibition Hall
(Old Fair), Charles-de-Gaulle-Platz, Köln | Cologne (H), Adolf Abel,
1927–28

Heilig-Kreuz-Kirche | Holy Cross Church, Bochumer Straße 113/117,
Gelsenkirchen (F), Josef Franke, 1927–29

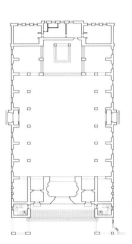

0   20

129

Turm Mutterhaus der Missionsschwestern vom Heiligsten Herzen
Jesu (Herz-Jesu-Krankenhaus) | Tower, Sacred Heart of Jesus Mis-
sionary Sisters' Mother House (Sacred Heart Hospital), Westfalen-
straße 109, Münster (I), 1930er? | 1930s?

130
Bettenturm Raphaelsklinik | Ward Tower Block, Raphael Hospital,
Windthorststraße 36, Münster (I), Carl Brocker, 1929–30

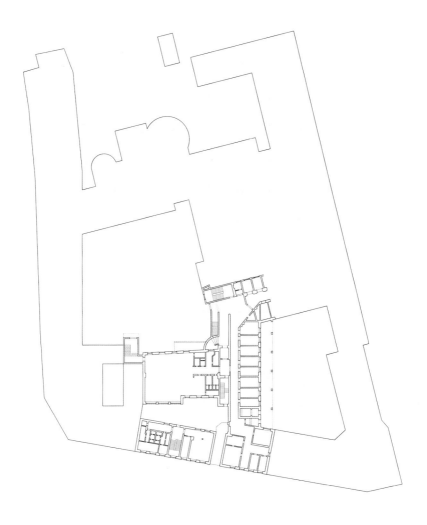

0   20

131
Rathaus | Town Hall, Schwartzstraße 72, Oberhausen (J), Ludwig
Freitag, 1927–30

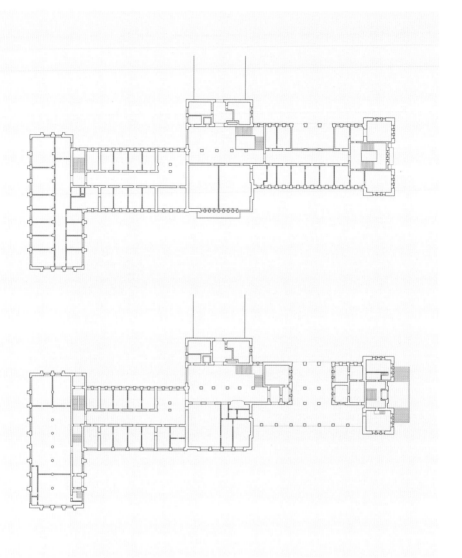

131
Rathaus | Town Hall, Schwartzstraße 72, Oberhausen (J), Ludwig
Freitag, 1927–30

132
Gär- und Lagerkeller Dortmunder Union Brauerei (Dortmunder U)
| Fermentation and Storage Cellar, Dortmund Union Brewery (Dort-
mund U), Leonie-Reygers-Terrasse, Dortmund (C), Emil Moog,
1926–27

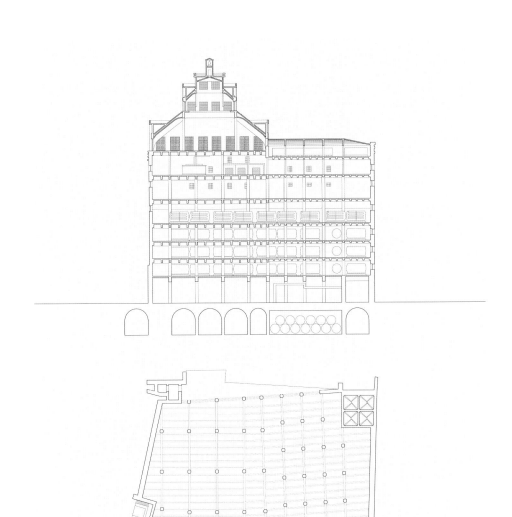

0   20

133
Hansaring-Hochhaus | Hansaring Highrise, Hansaring 97, Köln |
Cologne (H), Jacob Koerfer, 1924–25

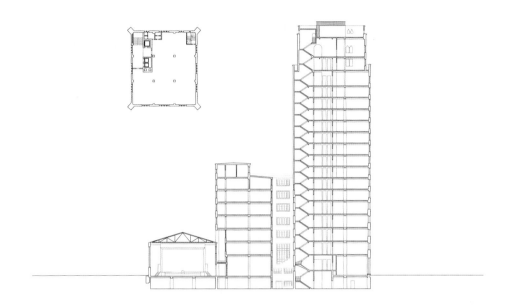

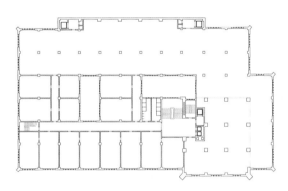

0   20

Hans-Sachs-Haus | Hans Sachs Building, Ebertstraße 15, Gelsen-
kirchen (F), Alfred Fischer, 1924–27

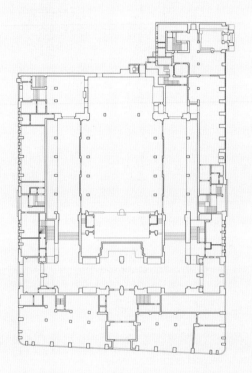

0   20

134
Hans-Sachs-Haus | Hans Sachs Building, Ebertstraße 15, Gelsen-
kirchen (F), Alfred Fischer, 1924–27

135
Wilhelm-Marx-Haus | Wilhelm Marx Building, Heinrich-Heine-
Allee 53, Düsseldorf (D), Wilhelm Kreis, 1921–24

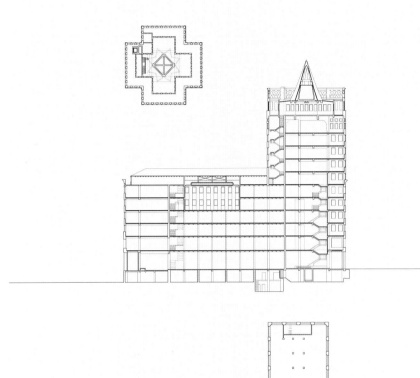

0 ⎿⎾�⌐⎿ 20 ⊖

136
GESOLEI Ehrenhof (Museum Kunstpalast) | GESOLEI Cour
d'honneur (Museum Kunstpalast), Ehrenhof 4–5, Düsseldorf (D),
Wilhelm Kreis, 1925–26

137
GESOLEI Rheinterrassen-Restaurant | GESOLEI Rhine Terrace
Restaurant, Joseph-Beuys-Ufer 33, Düsseldorf (D), Wilhelm Kreis,
1925–26

GESOLEI Reichsmuseum für Gesellschafts- und Wirtschaftskunde
(NRW-Forum Kultur und Wirtschaft) | GESOLEI National Museum
for Social and Economic Studies (NRW-Forum Culture and Economy),
Ehrenhof 2, Düsseldorf (D), Wilhelm Kreis, 1925–26

139
GESOLEI Rheinhalle (Tonhalle) | GESOLEI Rhine Hall (Düsseldorf
Concert Hall), Ehrenhof 1, Düsseldorf (D), Wilhelm Kreis, 1925–26

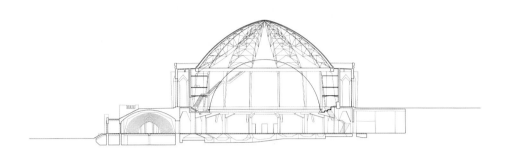

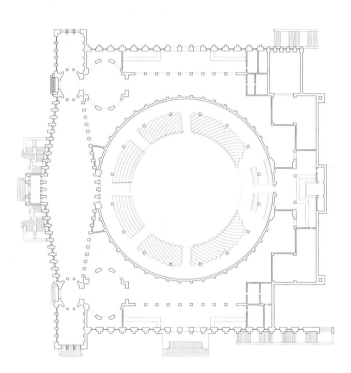

0   20

139
GESOLEI Rheinhalle (Tonhalle) | GESOLEI Rhine Hall (Düsseldorf
Concert Hall), Ehrenhof 1, Düsseldorf (D), Wilhelm Kreis, 1925–26

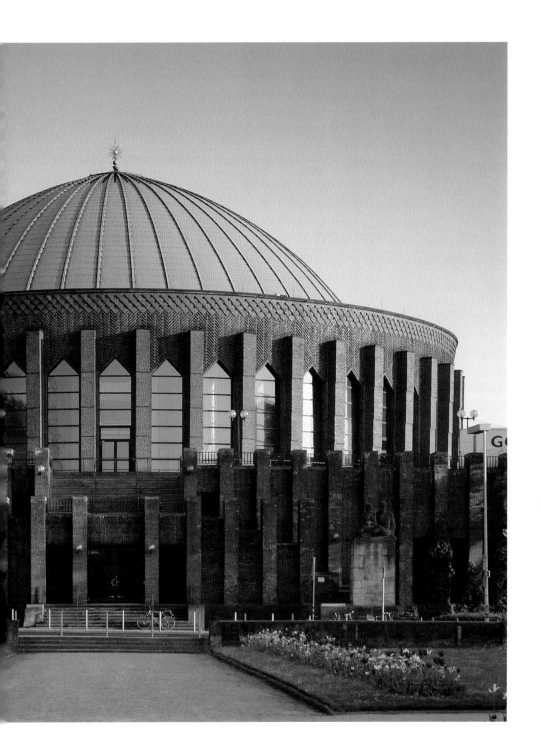

140

Allgemeine Ortskrankenkasse Wanne-Eickel | Wanne-Eickel Public
Health Insurance Company, Märkische Straße 11, Herne (F), Georg
Gobrecht, Ferdinand Revermann, 1927

141

Bauunternehmung Gebr. Meyer | Meyer Brothers Building Company,
Sachsenbergstraße 3, Köln | Cologne (H), 1920er? | 1920s?

142

Finanz- und Zollamt (Finanzamt Gelsenkirchen-Süd) | Tax and Cus-
toms Office (Gelsenkirchen South Tax Office), Zeppelinallee 9–13,
Gelsenkirchen (F), Alfred Reischig, 1928

143

Erweiterung und Umbau Gemeindehaus | Extension and Conversion,
Parish House, Bochumer Straße 165, Magdalenenstraße 1–5, Reck-
linghausen (A), 1927

144

Kiosk Wermelskirchen | Wermelskirchen Kiosk, Heiligenhoven,
Lindlar (bis | until 2010: Markt, Wermelskirchen) (A)

145

Polizeiamt Sterkrade | Sterkrade Police Station, Wilhelmplatz 2,
Oberhausen (A), Frenzel, 1925–27

146

Siedlung Heeper Fichten | Heeper Fichten Housing Estate, Adolf-
Damaschke-Straße 5–11, Althoffstraße 2–20, Bielefeld (A), Gustav
Vogt, 1925–26 (Wiederaufbau | Reconstruction 1948–49)

147

Siedlung Im Siekerfelde | Im Siekerfelde Housing Estate, Auf dem
Calvienenfelde 20–24, 25–27, Im Siekerfelde 2–24, Bielefeld (A),
Gustav Vogt, 1927–30

148

Spritzenhaus Sevinghausen | Sevinghausen Fire Station, Lohacker-straße 9, Bochum (A), ca. 1920

149

Torhaus Siedlung Königsbrügge | Gatehouse, Königsbrügge Housing Estate, Königsbrügge 32–33, Bielefeld (A), Friedrich Schultz, 1924

150

Umbau St. Johannes Baptist | Conversion, St John the Baptist, Bren-scheder Straße 43, Bochum (A), Anton Meister, 1930–32

151

Villa Böhme | Villa Böhme, Klinikstraße 87, Bochum (B), Heinrich Schmiedeknecht, 1927–28

152

Villa Nuphaus | Villa Nuphaus, Luise-Hensel-Straße 6, Bottrop (A), Josef Franke, 1926–27

153

Wohn- und Atelierhaus Edmund Körner | Edmund Körner's Resi-dence and Studio, Moltkestraße 50, Essen (E), Edmund Körner, ca. 1925

154

Wohnhäuser | Flats, Benrather Straße 1–3, Düsseldorf (D)

155

Wohnhäuser | Flats, Parkstraße 7, Schubertstraße 2–3, Wilhelmstraße 10, Herne (F)

KARTEN
GEBÄUDEREGISTER
ARCHITEKTEN

MAPS
INDEX OF BUILDINGS
ARCHITECTS

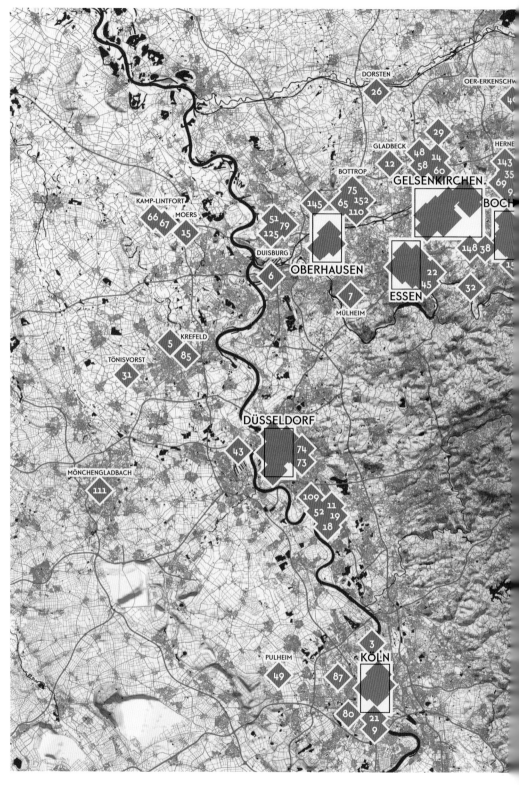

A   1, 3, 5, 6, 7, 8, 9, 10, 11, 12, 14, 15, 18, 19, 20, 21, 22, 24,
     26, 27, 29, 30, 31, 32, 35, 37, 38, 40, 42, 43, 45, 48, 49, 51,
     52, 58, 59, 60, 62, 65, 66, 67, 69, 73, 74, 75, 79, 80, 82, 85,
     86, 87, 93, 95, 96, 104, 109, 110, 111, 119, 125, 143, 144,
     145, 146, 147, 148, 149, 150, 152

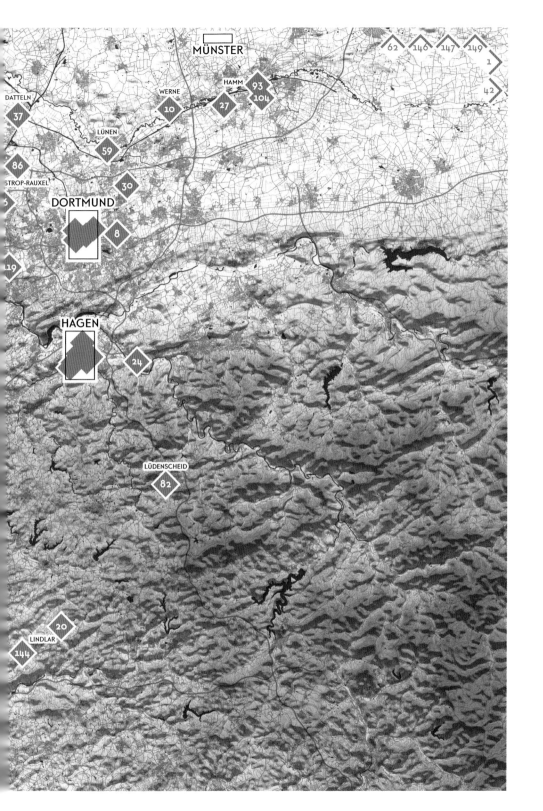

MÜNSTER

62 146 147 149
1

42

DATTELN

37

WERNE
10

HAMM
93
104
27

LÜNEN

59

86

STROP-RAUXEL

30

DORTMUND

8

19

HAGEN

24

LÜDENSCHEID

82

20

LINDLAR

144

0   10   20

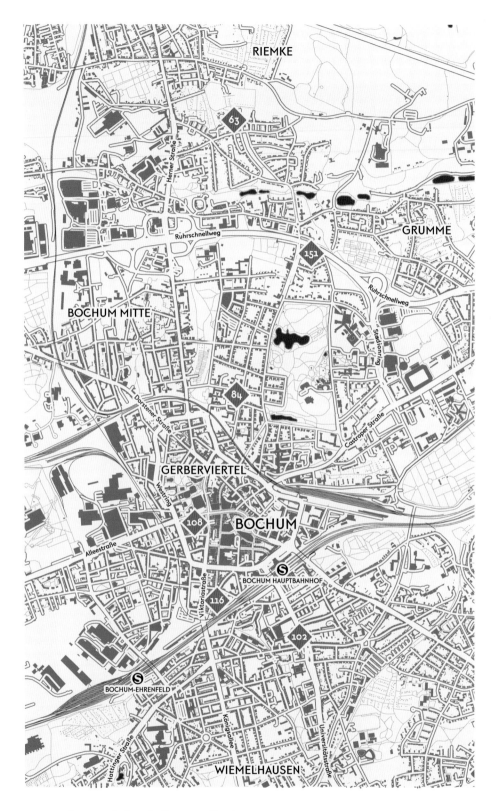

RIEMKE

63

GRUMME

Herner Straße

Ruhrschnellweg

151

BOCHUM MITTE

Ruhrschnellweg

Stadionring

84

Castroper Straße

Dorstener Straße

GERBERVIERTEL

Westring

108

BOCHUM

Alleestraße

S
BOCHUM HAUPTBAHNHOF

Viktoriastraße

116

102

S
BOCHUM-EHRENFELD

Hattinger Straße

Königsallee

Universitätsstraße

WIEMELHAUSEN

NORDMARKT-OST

Münsterstraße

Bornstraße

Borsigstraße

Brackeler Straße

Mallinckrodtstraße

Leopoldstraße

Heiligegartenstraße

Gronaustraße

Grüne Straße

56

DORTMUND
HAUPTBAHNHOF

Burgwall

132

DORTMUND

Hamburger Straße

Heiliger Weg

Möllerstraße

Hiltropwall

Süddwall

Ostwall

121

Hohe Straße

Ruhrallee

Märkische Straße

97
83

Lindemannstraße

Hohe Straße

RUHRALLE OST

Westfalendamm

Wittekindstraße

Rheinlanddamm

Ruhrallee

WESTFALENHALLE

Ardeystraße

SIGNAL IDUNA PARK

C   Dortmund 56, 83, 97, 121, 132   0   0,5   1,0

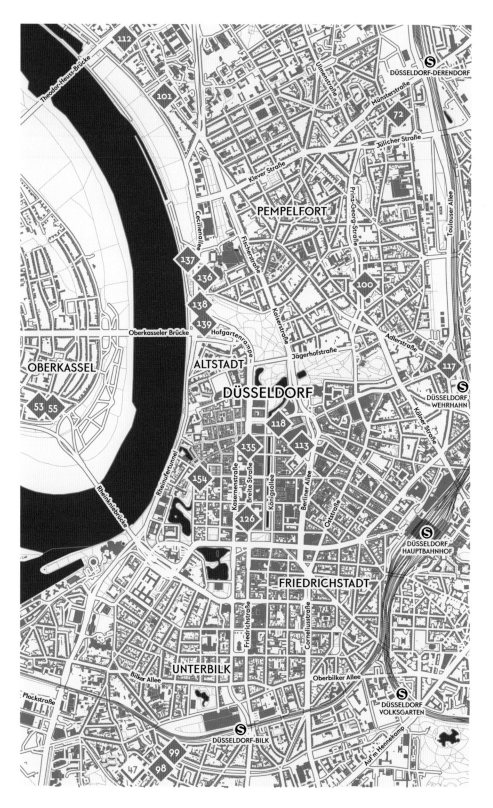

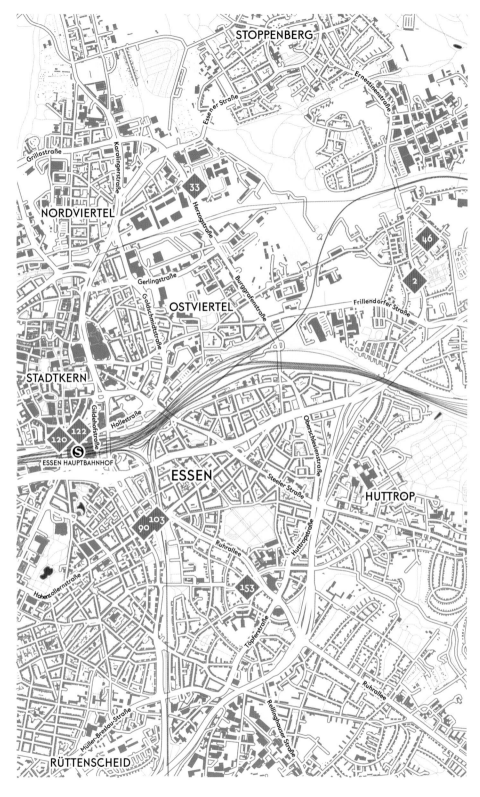

STOPPENBERG

Ernestinenstraße

Essener Straße

Grillostraße

Karolingerstraße

NORDVIERTEL

33

Herzogstraße

46

2

Gerlingstraße

Burggrafenstraße

Frillendorfer Straße

OSTVIERTEL

Goldschmidtstraße

STADTKERN

Gildehofstraße

Hollestraße

Oberschlesienstraße

120 122

S

ESSEN HAUPTBAHNHOF

ESSEN

Steeler Straße

HUTTROP

103

90

Ruhrallee

Huttropstraße

Hohenzollernstraße

153

Töpferstraße

Ruhrallee

Müller-Breslau-Straße

Rellinghauser Straße

RÜTTENSCHEID

E   Essen 2, 33, 46, 90, 103, 120, 122, 153   0   0,5   1,0

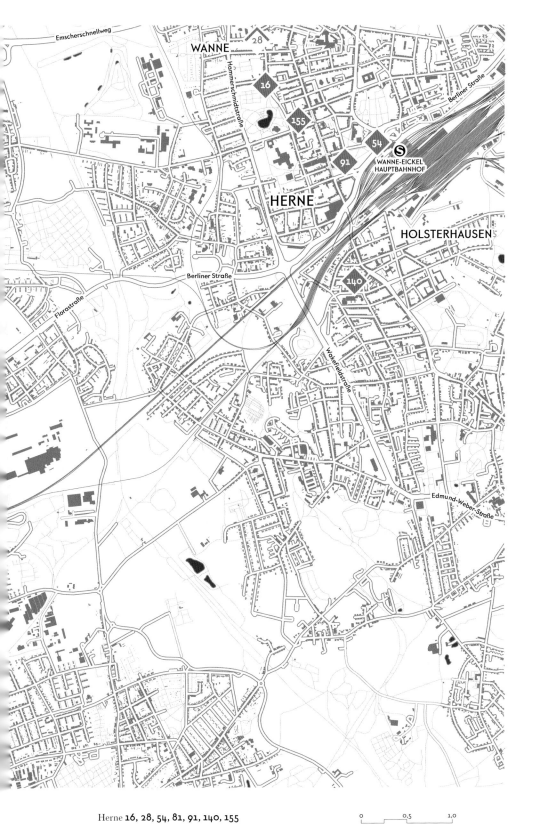

Herne **16, 28, 54, 81, 91, 140, 155**

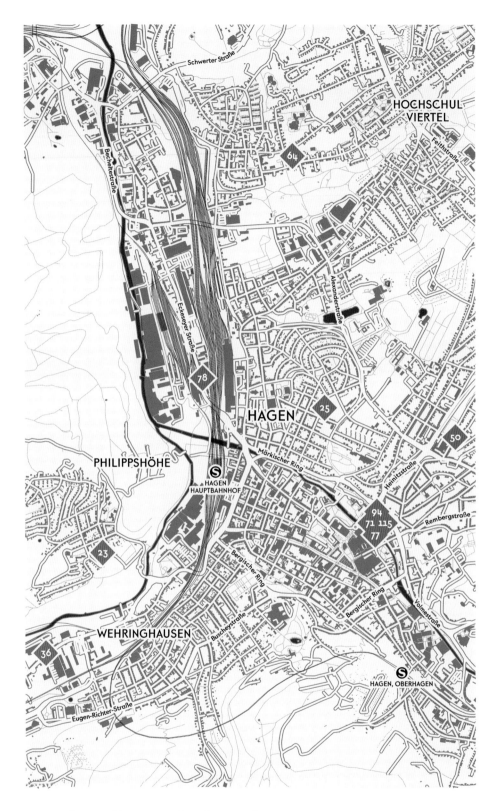

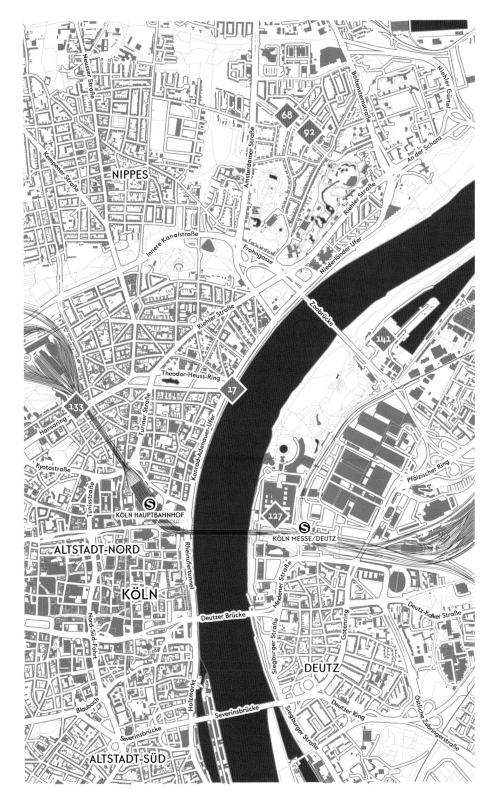

NEUSSER Straße
NIPPES
Kempener Straße
Innere Kanalstraße
Frohngasse
Amsterdamer Straße
68
92
An der Schanz
Niehler Gürtel
Boltensternstraße
Riehler Straße
Niederländer Ufer
Zoobrücke
141
Riehler Straße
Theodor-Heuss-Ring
17
133
Hansaring
Turiner Straße
Kyotostraße
Konrad-Adenauer-Ufer
Pfälzischer Ring
Tunisstraße
Rheinufertunnel
KÖLN HAUPTBAHNHOF
127
KÖLN MESSE/DEUTZ
ALTSTADT-NORD
KÖLN
Nord-Süd-Fahrt
Deutzer Brücke
Mindener Straße
Siegburger Straße
Gotenring
Deutz-Kalker Straße
DEUTZ
Deutzer Ring
Östliche Zubringerstraße
Blaubach
Holzmarkt
Severinsbrücke
Severinsbrücke
Siegburger Straße
ALTSTADT-SÜD

H   Köln | Cologne 17, 68, 92, 127, 133, 141   0   0,5   1,0

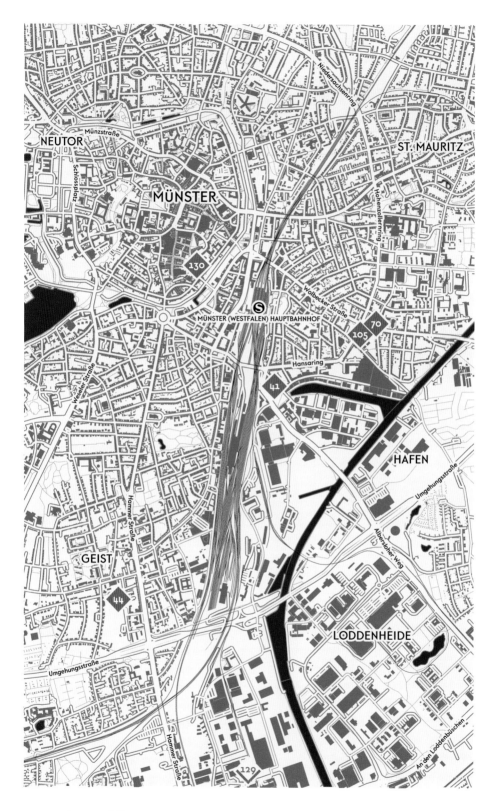

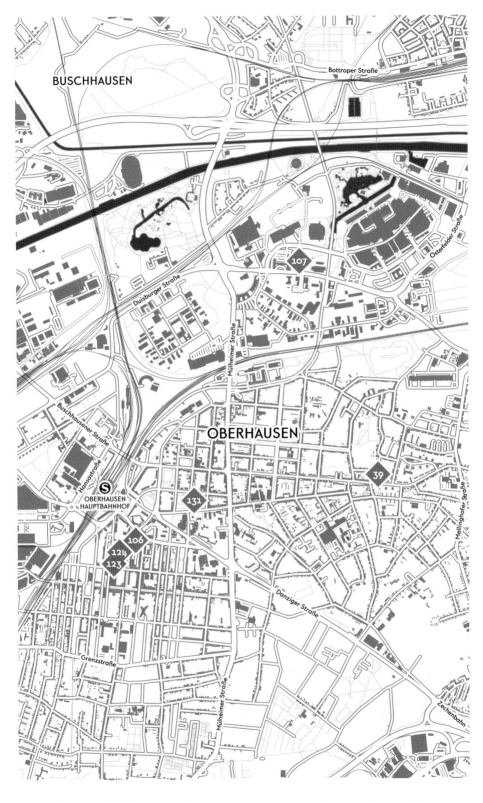

BUSCHHAUSEN

Bottroper Straße

Osterfelder Straße

107

Duisburger Straße

Mülheimer Straße

OBERHAUSEN

Buschhausener Straße

39

Mellinghofer Straße

Hansastraße

131

S OBERHAUSEN
HAUPTBAHNHOF

106
124
123

Danziger Straße

Grenzstraße

Mülheimer Straße

Zechenbahn

0   0,5   1,0

GEBÄUDEREGISTER

INDEX OF BUILDINGS

ARCHITEKTEN | ARCHITECTS

QUELLEN | SOURCES

Sämtliche Bilder sind in den Jahren 2010 und 2015 entstanden. Grundlage der Zeichnungen ist historisches Planmaterial aus Zeitschriften, Mongrafien und Archiven. Der ausgeführte wie auch heutige Zustand weicht deshalb mitunter von den Zeichnungen ab. Bei den Gebäudebezeichnungen werden historische Namen zuerst genannt, heutige stehen in Klammern. Die Daten geben den Bauzeitraum oder das Fertigstellungsjahr der Gebäude beziehungsweise relevanter Um- oder Anbauten an. Der Großbuchstabe in Klammern verweist auf die entsprechende Karte in diesem Buch. Sämtliche Daten wurden mit höchster Sorgfalt erhoben. Unsichere Angaben sind mit einem Fragezeichen gekennzeichnet. Architekt und Baujahr waren nicht in allen Fällen zu ermitteln; die Autoren bedanken sich vorab für ergänzende Hinweise.

All of the pictures were taken between 2010 and 2015. The drawings are based on historic material taken from periodicals, monographs or found in archives. The appearance of the buildings, either as they were built or as they stand today, may differ for this reason. The original names of the buildings are listed first, with current names following in brackets. The dates give the period of construction or the date of completion and those of any significant renovations or extensions. The capital letter in brackets refers to the relevant map in this book. Dates were sourced and scrutinised with the greatest care. Uncertain entries are marked with a question mark. The architect and year of completion were not always available; the authors offer thanks in advance for any information submitted.

Für Unterstützung bei der Recherche danken wir | We should like to express special thanks for research support to: Thorsten Brokmann (Untere Denkmalbehörde Stadt Herne), Ina Hanemann (Hagen), Henkel AG & Co. (Düsseldorf), Joachim Neuß (Untere Denkmalbehörde Stadt Dorsten), Thomas Nölleke (Münster), Gudrun Rapp (Untere Denkmalbehörde Stadt Moers).

LITERATUR | FURTHER READING

Bartmann, Ina: Das Henkel-Werk in Düsseldorf-Holthausen 1900–1940. Ein außergewöhnlicher Unternehmer und sein Architekt. Dissertation Bergische Universität Wuppertal 2008; Baukunst NRW, http://www.baukunst-nrw.de; Bergmann, Berger; Brdenk, Peter (Hg.|ed.): Architektur in Essen 1900–1960. Essen 2012; Bund Deutscher Architekten BDA, Gruppe Gelsenkirchen (Hg.|ed.): Gelsenkirchen. Architektur im Ruhrgebiet. Essen 1985; Busch, Wilhelm: Bauten der 20er Jahre an Rhein und Ruhr. Architektur als Ausdrucksmittel (Beiträge zu den Bau- und Kunstdenkmälern im Rheinland, Bd.|vol. 32). Köln | Cologne 1993; Denkmalliste Düsseldorf, https://inprobauauskunft.duesseldorf.de/ui.inpro/denkmal/search.jsf; Föhl, Axel: Architekturführer Ruhrgebiet. Berlin 2010; Funck, Britta: Wilhelm Riphahn. Architekt in Köln. Eine Bestandsaufnahme. Köln | Cologne 2004; Gottschlich, Peter; Kwiatkowski, Jürgen: Kamp-Lintfort. Menschen und Denkmäler. Erfurt 2007; Hanemann, Ina; Holtmann, Petra: Hagener Architektur. Hagen 1996; Hänsel, Sylvaine; Rethfeld, Stefan: Architekturführer Münster. Berlin 2008; Heuter, Christoph: Emil Fahrenkamp 1885–1966. Architekt im rheinisch-westfälischen Industriegebiet (Arbeitsheft der rheinischen Denkmalpflege, H.|no. 59). Petersberg 2002; Jordan, Rüdiger: Sakrale Baukunst in Bochum. Bochum 2003; Kanz, Roland; Wiener Jürgen (Hg.|ed.): Architekturführer Düsseldorf. Berlin 2001; Nerdinger, Winfried; Mai, Ekkehard (Hg.|ed.): Wilhelm Kreis. Architekt zwischen Kaiserreich und Demokratie 1873–1955. München | Munich 1994; Oberstadtdirektor der Stadt Herne; Bund Deutscher Architekten BDA, Bezirksgruppe Herne und Wanne-Eickel (Hg.|ed.): Herne Architekturführer. Herne 1987; Pankoke, Barbara: Der Essener Architekt Edmund Körner (1874–1940). Leben und Werk. Weimar 1996; Rescher, Holger: Backsteinarchitektur der 1920er Jahre in Düsseldorf. Dissertation Rheinische Friedrich-Wilhelms-Universität zu Bonn 2001; Stadt Oberhausen, Stadtbibliothek und Volkshochschule (Hg.|ed.): Bert-Brecht-Haus 1925 bis 2014: Ein Haus wird Kultur. Oberhausen 2014; Stommer, Rainer; Mayer-Gürr, Dieter: Hochhaus. Der Beginn in Deutschland. Marburg 1990; Voigt, Wolfgang; Flagge, Ingeborg: Dominikus Böhm 1880–1955. Tübingen/Berlin 2005; Wagner, Georg: Kommunalpolitik und Wohnungsbau in Bielefeld 1918–1960, in: Schulz, Günther (Hg.|ed.): Wohnungspolitik im Sozialstaat. Deutsche und europäische Lösungen 1918–1960. Düsseldorf 1993, S.|p. 71–102; Watzlawik, Sigrid: Visionen in Stein. Modernes Bauen in Essen 1910–1930. Essen 1998; Wegener, Maria: Der Architekt Josef Franke aus Gelsenkirchen (1876–1944). Dissertation Rheinische Friedrich-Wilhelms-Universität zu Bonn 1989.

DANKSAGUNG | ACKNOWLEDGEMENTS

Auch dieses Mal ist Fragments of Metropolis nur durch die Unterstützung großartiger Freunde und Förderer möglich geworden. Wieder haben sie Pläne gezeichnet, uns beim Layout unterstützt, die Texte übersetzt, das Buch während des Crowdfundings bekannter gemacht, mit finanziellen Zuwendungen den Druck des Buches ermöglicht, mit ihrem Enthusiasmus uns motiviert weiterzumachen. Danke!

Once again Fragments of Metropolis has only been made possible with the help of our extraordinary friends and supporters. They drew plans, helped us with the layouts, translated texts, spread the word during the crowdfunding campaign, and finally, continually motivated us with their enthusiasm. We thank all of you!

HAUPTFÖRDERER | PRINCIPAL SPONSOR

Kümmerlein Rechtsanwälte & Notare, Essen

FÖRDERER | SPONSORS

Keller AG Ziegeleien, Pfungen
Vivawest Wohnen GmbH, Gelsenkirchen

GÖNNER | SUPPORTERS

Daniel Behr
Daniel Boermann
Alexander Büchel
Cremer Wietersheim
Architekten, Berlin
Eva-Maria & Jens N. Daldrop
Bruno Fritschi
Christiane & Dietrich Goldmann
Elie G. Haddad
Jaap Janssen
Lilian & Lutz Kögler
Daniela Konrad
Petra & Olaf Lehmann

Friederike & Stephan Molls
Volker Mueller
Dennis Neu
nightnurse images, Zürich
Marc-Olivier Paux
Michael Rabe
Frauke Ries
Jutta Romberg
Daniel Romer
Fiona Scherkamp
Benjamin Sieber
Stefan Zappe
Clemens Zirkelbach

IMPRESSUM | IMPRINT

Hirmer Verlag GmbH
Nymphenburger Straße 84
80636 München | Munich

KONZEPT | CONCEPT
Christoph Rauhut, Niels Lehmann

GESTALTUNG | LAYOUT
Christoph Rauhut, Niels Lehmann

ÜBERSETZUNG | TRANSLATION
Philip Shelley

LEKTORAT | COPY-EDITING
Tanja Bokelmann

KORREKTORAT | PROOFREADING
Tanja Bokelmann (Deutsch), Jane Michael (English)

DRUCK, BINDUNG, LITHOGRAFIE | PRINTING, BINDING, LITHOGRAPHY
Westermann Druck, Zwickau

PAPIER | PAPER
Profi matt 150g/m²

SCHRIFTEN | TYPES
Koban 3000, BA13

ABBILDUNGEN | PICTURES
Fassadenstudie | Study for a façade: © Private Sammlung, Zürich
Alle weiteren Abbildungen | All other pictures: © Niels Lehmann

ZEICHNUNGEN | DRAWINGS
Dennis Ahrendt, Annina Baumgartner, Kristina Bindernagel, Daria Blaschkiewitz, Jens Daldrop, Jenny
Dittrich, Nicole Gamisch, Felix Greiner-Petter, Michael Grunitz, Andres Herzog, Niels Lehmann,
Stephan Liebscher, Ties Linders, Hannes Mahlknecht, Evgenia Pronina, Michael Rabe, Christoph
Rauhut, Jutta Romberg, Hannes Rutenfranz, Petra Schwyter, Nils Tennhoff, Florian Summa, Clemens
Wagner, Christine Wilkening-Aumann, Karl Wruck

KARTEN | MAPS
© OpenStreetMap und Mitwirkende, CC-BY-SA

2. überarb. Auflage 2016   ISBN 978-3-7774-2772-0
(1. Auflage 2016   ISBN 978-3-7774-2567-2)
© 2016 Hirmer Verlag GmbH, München | Munich; Christoph Rauhut; Niels Lehmann

www.hirmerverlag.de | www.hirmerpublishers.com
www.fragmentsofmetropolis.eu

Biliografische Information der Deutschen Nationalbibliothek
Die Deutsche Nationalbibliothek verzeichnet diese Publikation in der Deutschen Nationalbibliografie;
detaillierte bibliografische Daten sind im Internet über http://dnb.d-nb.de abrufbar.

Biliographic Information published by the Deutsche Nationalbibliothek
The Deutsche Nationalbibliothek lists this publication in the Deutschen Nationalbibliografie; detailed
bibliographic data is available on the internet at http://dnb.d-nb.de.